The Earl

David Crock

...nnessee

Christmas 2023
For Connor
Love, Grammy and George

Published by Mission Point Press
2554 Chandler Rd.
Traverse City, MI 49696
(231) 421-9513
www.MissionPointPress.com

ISBN 978-1-961302-20-4
Library of Congress Control Number 2023917815

Printed in the United States of America

The Early Life and Times of

David Crockett

in East Tennessee

A lifelong study
By Joe Swann

MISSION POINT PRESS

Table of Contents

Preface

On Monday, May 30, 1955, I was one of hundreds of children in tow, lined up with our parents in a tunnel under the city sidewalks of downtown Knoxville, Tennessee. We children could look up to see the bottoms of shoes tramping across the metal grates on the sidewalk above us. The tunnel led to Miller's department-store basement where the actor Fess Parker was holding audience, preparing to receive his young fans in his role as the frontiersman Davy Crockett.

We kids were in awe of Fess Parker, who as the Walt Disney version of Davy Crockett, stood in his buckskin clothes and coonskin cap, holding his Kentucky long rifle. Like many boys in my generation, I was a certified Crockett fanatic. I had the coonskin cap, the rifle, the tomahawk, and the rubber skinning knife. I even had a commemorative Davy Crockett hot chocolate mug. If I wasn't outside reenacting Crockett's adventures, I could be found in my room, listening to my vinyl record of *The Ballad of Davy Crockett*, sung by Fess Parker himself, playing it over and over.

In this department-store basement, my mother stood patiently in line with my starstruck five-year-old self. We shuffled along in line, and I craned my neck for my first glimpse, close up and in person, of the face of Davy Crockett. As Fess Parker portrayed him, I thought of Crockett as reborn living legend—the most interesting person in the universe. At age five, this was certainly the most monumental thing I'd yet experienced in my young life.

When the line moved and our turn came, I looked up into the face of the tall, young, and handsome Fess Parker. I looked at the long and beautiful flintlock rifle at his side. "Crockett" extended his hand and I shook it. He looked just like I imagined he would. In a way, the event felt more real than anything I'd experienced in my young life so far. To this day, the memories of that encounter with Fess Parker as Davy Crockett have stayed with me. It was a treasured part of my childhood experiences and was undiminished by the fact that I was one of hundreds of children also meeting him that day. It was a moment I would never forget.

Even at that early age, I understood that David Crockett had been a real man, and that the Disney/Fess Parker version of Davy Crockett was a legend *about* that man. Still, I cherish my memories of the Disney Davy Crockett—his impression is imprinted on me and lives on through my enduring love of history, the frontier life, and the iconic firearms of the period. As I grew, my interest in the frontier and the west also grew to include characters like the Lone Ranger and Roy Rogers, who I emulated with my Fanner 50 cowboy pistol (a cap gun, really) and leather holster on my hip.

The destiny of the true-life David Crockett (1786–1836) would include becoming one of our first national celebrities. As a rugged frontiersman, Crockett symbolized a new kind of uniquely *American* man. When his life was cut short by his chance decision to fight at the Battle of the Alamo in February and March of 1836, he became a legend.

For a person who loves history, my mission to better understand Crockett and his old guns has been a wonderful adventure. I have tried to learn as much about David's life as possible, focusing on his early times in East Tennessee. It is my hope that by exploring the life of the historical Crockett, his contemporaries, and the landscapes on which he walked, we might gain a better sense of why his persona and his life's story have been so compelling to America and the world. Crockett has enjoyed nearly two hundred years of popularity as America's first homegrown celebrity and remains a unique and enduring American icon.

Personal Connections with Crockett

As I matured, I came to discover that I had a real-life connection to David Crockett. My father told stories about our ancestors, who lived in the same region as Crockett and knew him. My father's stories ignited my curiosity about Crockett's history and our relationship to him, and I was surprised to find out how much of Crockett's world and my own world overlapped.

I would describe our family's connection with David Crockett by first telling you about my father, Eugene Swann (1907–1976). Dad grew up in a house built in the 1850s in Dandridge, Tennessee, by his great-uncle, Samuel Scott McCuistion (1817–1893). The old house has been well maintained over its 170-plus years, thanks to loving owners who shared an appreciation of history and the past. Great-uncle Sam McCuistion had built the house adjacent to a sinkhole, which always intrigued me as a child. The cave-like opening seemed a call to exploration, and my parents were constantly warning my brother and me to keep out of it. The sinkhole might have been seen as a beneficial feature: in the days before septic tanks and sewer systems, the sinkhole offered a solution to the age-old problem of waste disposal.

Our family of four would make a seventy-mile round trip from our home in Maryville, Tennessee, to the town of Dandridge to visit my grandmother almost every weekend. As the seat of Jefferson County, the historic town of Dandridge is one of the three oldest towns in Tennessee: Jonesboro being recognized as the oldest, with Rogersville and Dandridge vying for second-place honors. My grandmother lived in one of Dandridge's oldest homes, about two blocks from the Jefferson County Courthouse.

It was during this time that Walt Disney created a national and global sensation by premiering its miniseries, *Davy Crockett*, starring Fess Parker in the title role, with Buddy Ebsen as Crockett's friend, George Russel. On a trip to Dandridge to visit my grandmother, my father, impressed by my intense fascination with Crockett, began telling me about our family's connections with the early frontiersman. He told me about our McCuistion ancestors, who had lived on Long

Creek about ten miles west of Dandridge and were neighbors of Davy Crockett when he lived there.

Much discussion has occurred over the years about whether Crockett ever went by the name "Davy." The popularization of the nickname Davy began with the Almanacs of the late 1830s and 1840s. Disney added fuel to the fire with its blockbuster *Davy Crockett* television shows. It is clear that he most often signed his name "David" or "D. Crockett," although his early signatures look at first glance like they are signed "Davie." However, after seeing the letter "d" in Crockett's other handwritten documents, it is clear that the last letter is a "d," not an "e." In one personal account written in the 1880s by an early East Tennessee neighbor of Crockett, he is referred to in dialog as "Davy."[1] But this account came almost fifty years after David's death, and the historical David Crockett had been popularized to such a degree that the name "Davy Crockett" was conditioned into the public consciousness.

My father recounted that his great-great-grandfather, James McCuistion, ran a country store at Long Creek. McCuistion's store was located 1.8 miles south of the Crockett home at Finley Gap, and a mile north of the present-day junction of Interstates 40 and 81. Crockett had been a regular customer at McCuistion's store. My father told of Crockett leaving Jefferson County, headed for middle Tennessee around 1811. Crockett owed James McCuistion a sum of money for goods he'd purchased at McCuistion's store. In lieu of tender, Crockett settled his account by giving James McCuistion one of his rifles in payment.

The Crockett rifle later passed from my third great-grandfather, James McCuistion, to his son, Major Samuel Scott McCuistion (who was my father's great-uncle, and in whose home his mother, Nina Gwinn Swann, resided). Nina Gwinn Swann lived in that house (built around 1850) until her death in 1963. The old house still stands (as of 2020). My father's uncle, Sam Gwinn, inherited the Crockett rifle,

---

1   "Connie's Corner Odds and Ends," *Morristown Gazette*, September 4, 1962.

being the only male heir of age, and took it with him when he moved to Goodwell, Oklahoma, as a railroad agent in the late 1890s. My father recalled at the age of nine traveling to Oklahoma by train in 1916 to see his Uncle Sam. My father had asked to see the rifle while he was there. His uncle had a hard time finding it, but eventually "dug around for a considerable time in an old smokehouse where he found it." Dad said the rifle was in "pretty rough shape," but he never forgot about the experience of getting to see and hold a rifle that had actually been owned by David Crockett.

For a time between 1930 and 1950, Sam Gwinn loaned the Crockett rifle to the Panhandle Museum in Goodwell, Oklahoma, where it appeared on exhibit. After Sam Gwinn's death, his only grandson (my cousin) inherited the rifle. In 1978, I made an offer to buy the rifle from my cousin, who accepted my offer. After acquiring the rifle, I began the process of having it restored.

During the process of restoring the Crockett rifle, it was a surprise to find the number of records that existed for this old gun. It had been documented through a number of sources, and the records clarified the Crockett connection quite readily. In fact, I found that historical information on the rifle was often easier to find than reliable information about Crockett's early life in East Tennessee.

After having the Crockett rifle restored, I put it on loan to the Tennessee State Museum in Nashville, where it was on display for about ten years from 1979 to 1990. The rifle made a trip to Washington, DC, in 1986, where it was displayed along with Crockett's 1806 marriage license at the Smithsonian Institution's National Portrait Gallery as part of an exhibit celebrating Crockett's two hundredth birthday. Today, the restored Crockett rifle can be seen at the Museum of East Tennessee History in Knoxville, where it has been on loan since 1995.

Introduction

Fifty years after the Declaration of Independence, much of America was still sorting out what it meant to be an American. A Tennessee frontiersman, statesman, and folk hero named David Crockett was one of the first personalities to capture the imagination of the American people: first with his rugged woodsman persona, later with his "gentleman from the cane" entrance onto the stage of national politics, and ultimately with his death at the iconic Battle of the Alamo.

David Crockett (1786–1836) was born an obscure middle son of nine children. The family, led by an alcoholic and bad-luck father, lived poor and on the dangerous edge of the American frontier. How did a person so off the beaten path become a household name that has continued to resonate for nearly two hundred years?

Crockett's legend can be attributed in part to the profitability of publishing in the young nation. By the early 1830s, the popular press began to reach a large portion of the United States. An early biography of Crockett was published anonymously and was thought to have been authored by Crockett himself. Titled *The Life and Adventures of Colonel David Crockett of West Tennessee* and published in 1833, the book was later determined to have been written by Matthew St. Clair Clarke (1790–1852), a congressional colleague of Crockett's when the Tennessee woodsman was serving as a congressman from Tennessee. It's believed that Clarke, elected seven times as clerk of the US House of Representatives, took the colorful recounting of stories told by Crockett himself, likely told at a Washington boardinghouse where a number of legislators lived while congress was in session. Clarke apparently augmented Crockett's stories by adding research from newspaper articles and personal visits to Crockett's home.

Clarke wrote the book anonymously, had it copyrighted by his associate James Strange French, and published it to considerable success.[2]

Political motivation was assumed to be one incentive behind Clarke's writing of the Crockett biography. The unauthorized biography was complimentary of Crockett and thought by later historians to be Clarke's attempt to bolster Crockett's reputation with the Whig party, formed in opposition to President Andrew Jackson, with whom Crockett had many conflicts. Clarke later republished the *Life and Adventures* in 1847 under the title of *Sketches and Eccentricities of Colonel David Crockett of West Tennessee*[3] (referred to hereafter as *Sketches*).

Clarke embellished the stories about Crockett, however, and retold them in a way that Crockett felt did not do justice to his original tales of his frontier life. Crockett also noted the financial success being enjoyed by Clarke with the strong sales of Crockett's unauthorized biography. American readers at the time showed great interest in stories of the young country's early frontier period, as demonstrated by the huge success of James Fenimore Cooper's popular Leatherstocking Tales: *The Pioneers* (1823), *The Last of the Mohicans* (1826), *The Prairie* (1827), *The Pathfinder* (1840), and *The Deerslayer* (1841).

The popularity of Clarke's book thus led Crockett to write his own book a year later, the autobiographical *A Narrative of the Life of David Crockett, of the State of Tennessee*, which he published in 1834. In his own account (authored with at least some editorial assistance from Thomas Chilton, a congressional colleague from Kentucky), Crockett gave a self-effacing, detailed, first-person look at his life up to that point. Telling his stories in his own way, Crockett saw his book as a

---

2   Arpad, Joseph John. ed. *A Narrative of the Life of David Crockett of the State of Tennessee* (New Haven, CT: College & University Press, 1972).

3   Clarke, Matthew St. Clair (probable author). *Sketches and Eccentricities of Colonel David Crockett of West Tennessee* (usual title) (New York: J. & J. Harper, 1833). Reprint of *The Life and Adventures of Colonel David Crockett of West Tennessee* (Cincinnati: "For the Proprietor," 1833).

way to capitalize on his growing popularity as a political figure, an American storyteller, and a humorist.

Referred to hereafter as his *Narrative*, Crockett's autobiography chronicled his remarkable life story of hard knocks and lessons learned from extreme poverty and the difficulties of living at the bottom of the social order on the hazardous edge of the American frontier. A remarkable feature of the *Narrative* is Crockett's memory for the details of people, places, and events that had taken place twenty-five to thirty-five years earlier. His ability to recall things such as distances have been checked and are often correct to the exact distance today. Accounts of people and events have been verified dozens of times and confirmed as accurate.

Numerous references to East Tennessee people in the *Narrative* have been examined. In not one instance can I document David's invention of fictitious characters for the purpose of advancing his views. Incidents that might seem contrived have been substantiated, such as his father's forgive-and-forget attitude toward the boy after he returned from a runaway trip to Virginia, or young Crockett being jilted by his first fiancée because he overindulged at a frolic and arrived two days late for his own wedding. Crockett's *Narrative* proves to be scrupulous in his commitment to honesty and his ability to remember precise details and events.

Crockett's *Narrative* is also an important record of a time and place in American history when the country was defining itself as a nation and a people. Crockett's is the record of an era when many unique and interesting individuals from the Tennessee frontier country would play out high-stakes dramas that would set a pattern for future western expansion. The big winners of the dramas of land acquisition were a few canny, opportunistic land speculators with access to capital or credit, who almost always had undeclared conflicts of interest and used their influence and/or political positions to feather their own nests. The big losers of America's western expansion were of course the Native Americans who'd lived on the land for thousands of years.

Crockett's tough upbringing on the Tennessee frontier forged in him a strength of character. He earned a seat in Congress, where he dared to challenge the most powerful and vengeful man in America—fellow Tennessean and American president Andrew Jackson. Crockett's stand against Jackson's top priority legislation—the Indian Removal Act— put him forever at odds with the president. In taking this stand for the rights of Native peoples, Crockett stood alone: he was the only representative from the western districts of the United States to oppose Jackson on Indian removal. This act forced the few remaining Native peoples out of their homelands, making way for the implacable expansion of the boundaries of the United States.

Crockett's surprising dark-horse ascendance to a seat in the US House of Representatives combined with the publication of his autobiographical frontier *Narrative* ignited a fascination with Crockett, which took root in the culture and consciousness of America. Crockett began the process of endearing himself to successive generations with his engaging wit and humor. The persevering spirit forged on the land of eastern Tennessee carried him through his many struggles in the halls of congress, and the stories of his early life struck a chord with Americans of that era. Crockett began from a humble station and possessed a compelling humanity and character that enabled him to rise above the lowly upbringing (much like Abraham Lincoln, who would serve Illinois in the US Congress a decade later). Crockett became, arguably, America's first national celebrity and a symbol of an emerging national identity.

Many contemporary historians agree that any study of Crockett, whether his life or his legend, begins with his autobiography. In *Davy Crockett: A Handbook*, Richard Hauck described the *Narrative* as helpful to understand the differences between the two Crocketts, the man and the legend. Hauck wrote that Crockett's *Narrative* was "the foundation of his legend [and] can be considered the definitive map of the two regions which constitute Crockett country."[4] Historical work

---

4   Richard Boyd Hauck, *Davy Crockett: A Handbook* (Lincoln: University of Nebraska Press, 1982 & 1986), 134.

that expands our understanding of the *Narrative* is important to both fields of study.

Crockett's autobiography is an enduring gift, telling of the life of a strong young man on the edge of a great and sometimes terrible frontier as America pushed west. David saw himself as the product of his heritage and not the creator of a new one. His self-concept and success were derived from the esteem of friends and supporters, which provided him with an inner strength and confidence in himself. Crockett's wit, humor, and natural leadership, along with his solid abilities as a frontier citizen, gained him the trust and support of his friends, neighbors, and constituents. His remarkably straightforward account of his tribulations in this land of opportunity and peril is an important contribution to the understanding of early American life and history.

After Crockett's death at the Alamo in 1836, the frontiersman myth of Davy Crockett expanded, with nearly thirty books published about him from 1839 to 1955. Walter Blair's 1940 article, "Six Davy Crocketts,"[5] argued that the real Davy Crockett was unknowable because so much fictitious information about him had been woven into the fabric of his real life's history. Blair held that an untangling of the real Crockett from the legendary Crockett was impossible and his historical legacy was unrecoverable.

That mythologized version of Crockett's life was reintroduced to American culture fifteen years after Blair's article when Walt Disney broadcast the short-lived series, *Davy Crockett*, which ran only five episodes between 1954 and 1955. Starring Fess Parker as the iconic Tennessee woodsman, the series elevated the name of Crockett and led to a generation of American youngsters idolizing the lanky, handsome hero.

Crockett's place as a hero in American lore is unique. Where figures like Paul Bunyan or Pecos Bill are wholly fictional, David Crockett was a real historical figure who became a legendary figure whose life was in part fictionalized: a historical man who became an enduring

---

5   Walter Blair, "Six Davy Crocketts." *Southwest Review* 25 (1940).

American icon who straddles both the historical and fictional realms. Several Crockett writers have suggested that the actual events of Crockett's life are not as important nor as interesting as is the legend. At the heart of this argument is the question about the importance of Crockett's impact on important issues of his day, and whether his lasting legacy resulted from his political efforts and accomplishments— or simply from the legendary tales.

But from the accounts of the people who actually knew Crockett, one gets the picture of a man who was a magnetic, charismatic, and fun-loving *gentleman from the cane*: an authentic American product. Crockett's unapologetic frontier style was in contrast to the Europeanized Americans who came before him.

Shackford's Biography

In 1956, a year after the broadcast of the Disney television series *Davy Crockett*, a seminal history book appeared on bookstore shelves. Published posthumously by Dr. James Atkins Shackford of North Carolina State University, *David Crockett: The Man and the Legend* provided a starting point for the serious academic study of the historical Crockett. While nearly three dozen books had been published on Crockett's life since his autobiographical *Narrative* appeared more than a century prior,[6] it was Shackford's biography that captured an accurate and credible image of Crockett. Shackford set out to show that the historical Crockett was, in fact, knowable through at least one reliable source: Crockett's own autobiography. Dr. Shackford, whose death in 1953 preceded the printing of his authoritative work on Crockett, had also been working on an annotated edition of Crockett's *Narrative*.

In *The Man and the Legend*, Shackford analyzed information on David's early life to make comparisons with Crockett's accounts of

---

6   Bibliography on Works on David Crockett, Wikipedia entry. Accessed January 4, 2021. https://en.wikipedia.org/wiki/Bibliography_of_works_on_Davy_Crockett

his life events and legitimized the *Narrative* as a valuable and accurate record of the events surrounding Crockett's life. While the first third of Crockett's *Narrative* chronicled his early years, Shackford described what he felt was a dearth of historical information available on Crockett's early life, saying: "The annals of David Crockett's life prior to his twelfth year are practically confined to half the length of a poor man's tombstone."[7]

Some Crockett scholarship has repeated the theme that the historical life of David Crockett is less interesting or important than the *legend* of Davy Crockett. In *Davy Crockett: A Handbook*, Dr. Richard Hauck contended that Dr. Shackford's motivation to research the life of Crockett stemmed more from Crockett's fame as a legend than it did from any importance or impact of Crockett on the tangible struggles of his time.[8]

Shackford in fact does highlight the historical importance of Crockett and his well-deserved spot in early American iconography. In Shackford's appendix to *David Crockett: The Man and the Legend*, the scholar gives his conclusions about the historical accuracies of the accounting Crockett gave for himself in his *Narrative*, differentiating the man from the legend:

> When one compares the authentic records about Crockett with his autobiographical account of them, only two sorts of discrepancies are found: first, a few additions, and slight deliberate alterations which I have attributed to the fact that David was still in politics and intended the *Autobiography* partially as campaign literature; and second, errors not in fact but in accuracy of dating fact, attributable obviously to its having been written entirely from memory. However, the rest of it is meticulously accurate, as established by parallel

---

7   James A. Shackford, *David Crockett: The Man and the Legend*, ed. John B. Shackford (Chapel Hill: University of North Carolina Press, 1956), 8.

8   Hauck, *Davy Crockett: A Handbook*, 135.

surviving records, that the only conclusion can be that, in content, the work is all David's own.[9]

Other works investigating the life of this American icon followed. More than a decade after Shackford's death, his work was continued and expanded upon by Stanley J. Folmsbee of the University of Tennessee. In an annotated facsimile edition, Folmsbee's *A Narrative of the Life of David Crockett of the State of Tennessee*[10] was published in 1973. The following decades would see dozens of books published on Crockett's life, from scholars like Michael Lofaro, William Groneman, and Michael Wallis.

Intro Summary

Growing up in eastern Tennessee would give David Crockett a strength of character that would demonstrate itself repeatedly over his short life. While serving in Congress, Crockett would author a Tennessee Land Bill (1829–1830), which gave rights to western Tennessee homesteaders who had been thrown off land they had cultivated for years but never officially deeded. He opposed Andrew Jackson in that president's support of the 1830 Indian Removal Act, which pushed southern Indian tribes to land west of the Mississippi. His flashes of the magnetism and willingness to advocate for the common man served to catapult David Crockett to national icon status.

The notoriety of Crockett's convictions resonated throughout cities as well as the frontier—he walked the walk and talked the talk of everyday, even downtrodden, Americans. Crockett stood by those convictions to the end of both his political career and his natural life.

A maxim attributed to Crockett was, "Be always sure you are right

---

9   Shackford, *David Crockett: The Man and the Legend*, 264–273.

10   Crockett, David. *A Narrative of the Life of David Crockett of the State of Tennessee* (Philadelphia: Carey & Hart, 1834). Facsimile edition with annotations and introduction, ed. James A. Shackford and Stanley J. Folmsbee (Knoxville: University of Tennessee Press, 1973).

and then go ahead." But most of the time it seemed that David would "go ahead" come hell or high water. Perhaps the man is best summarized in his own words, delivered to Congress upon his departure in 1835: "I told the people of my district that I would serve them as faithfully as I had done; but if not, they might go to hell, and I would go to Texas."

Go to Texas, Crockett did. Upon his arrival, he had choices to make. He could join Sam Houston in San Antonio, or he could go to the Alamo, a bastion in the war for Texas's independence from Mexico. It is possible that David saw an opportunity for glory at the Alamo and perhaps to recover some of his reputation after his stinging loss in the recent congressional election. Another potential explanation for Crockett's decision to go to the Alamo was that he had aligned himself with the Whig party. With Sam Houston in charge in San Antonio, Crockett may have seen that city as full of his political opponents. Crockett's affinity for autonomy and action over teamwork and hierarchy would cost him his life when the Alamo was overrun by Mexican troops in February and March of 1836.

The odds were long of the young David Crockett becoming a person singled out to be one of America's most recognized figures in history, culture, and politics. As he matured and moved west, his talents as an entertaining storyteller combined with his reliability and prowess as a hunter and woodsman started to earn him a reputation as an interesting person of character and ability, which sparked the imagination of a newly emerging American culture looking for its identity.

The size and scope of all that is Crockett has been, and continues to be, an evolutionary process. David's two hundredth birthday in 1986 ignited another revival of interest in Crockett topics. For more than two hundred years, a variety of writers, scholars, folklorists, literary and music historians, sociologists, painters and artists, and song writers continue to be drawn to Crockett. He has been examined from many perspectives as both the man and the legend.

In this work, I have dug deeply into Crockett's *Narrative* autobiography as it relates to the first half of his life, a period from 1786 to

1812, a period during which the state of Tennessee had its more formative influence on him. This book looks more closely at those formative years of Crockett's life, the influences of his Scots-Irish heritage, and the effect on his character of growing up as a frontiersman primarily in East Tennessee. The book ends with Crockett's move from Jefferson County to the Duck and Elk River area of Lincoln County, Tennessee, in late 1811 and early 1812, when Crockett was age twenty-six.

The early years shape the man. By understanding the landscape and culture of eastern Tennessee and how the landscape of that state helped shape Crockett, we hope to gain some insight into the character of a man who would stand up against a president's abuse of Native peoples, advocate for his constituents whether they were wealthy or poor and, in the end, fight a foreign army against insuperable odds, an effort that would cost him his life. This book examines that early period of Crockett's life to gain an understanding of how a poor boy from the edge of the American frontier became a storyteller, soldier, folk hero, congressman, and American cultural icon for the ages.

CHAPTER 1:

Crockett and His Rifles

Crockett/McCuistion/Swann Rifle. .49-caliber flintlock, Pennsylvania-made, ca. 1780–1800.

> *"I had by this time got to be mighty fond of the rifle, and had bought a capital one. I most generally carried her with me wherever I went, and though I had got back to the old Quaker's to live, who was a very particular man, I would sometimes slip out and attend the shooting matches, where they shot for beef; I always tried, though, to keep it a secret from him."*
>
> —From *A Narrative of the Life of David Crockett of the State of Tennessee* (*Narrative*), page 51.

The story of a frontier icon like David Crockett could rightly start with a chapter on the American long rifle. It was the rifle that became known as the *Kentucky Rifle* that helped win American independence, and it was the Kentucky rifle that enabled westward expansion of the young nation beginning in the late 1700s, providing meat for the table and protection on the frontier. The rifle was an indispensable tool for families moving west, and it was an important tool for Crockett.

And it was one rifle in particular—a Kentucky rifle once owned by David Crockett, which came into the McCuistion/Swann family—that created a tangible link to Crockett. The rifle is the reason we're here together in this book.

The Long Rifle as a Primary Wilderness Tool

The Kentucky rifle was one of the primary tools necessary for survival in the wilderness. The western frontier demanded a more accurate weapon than the heavy, smooth-bored muskets that were accurate up to a range of only about forty yards. While the older-designed muskets were less expensive to manufacture and maintain (which is why they remained in wide military use until after the Civil War), the downside was in the weight and accuracy. A ball spit from the smooth bore of a musket often missed its target, lacking the spin provided by the spiral-grooved "rifled" barrel, which caused the ball to fly straight. The innovation of a longer and rifled barrel was a development that improved both the accuracy and the effective range of these guns. While rifles took longer to reload, accuracy was valued more than rapid fire. On the frontier, an accurate shot could mean the difference between eating and going hungry, or even the difference between life and death.

Because these rifles were carried almost everywhere the owner went, craftsmen responded with rifles that were lighter, yet as durable as possible. These more-graceful rifles with thinner and longer barrels were a technological advancement over the heavier, thick-barreled *jaeger* hunting rifles built predominantly by German gunsmiths. Competition for willing buyers led gunsmiths to embellish these longer, lighter rifles with finely crafted, relief-carved curly maple stocks, brass patch boxes, brass butt plates, trigger guards, ramrod ferrule nose caps, or silver inlays. These rifles took on a delicate, streamlined appearance that was both functional and pleasing to the eye, and a representation of its owner's status. While these guns were the product of market demand, they were more than just a tool—a finely crafted flintlock long rifle became a part of its owner's identity and reputation and stood out as a thing of striking beauty and mechanical excellence. The long rifle was a frontiersman's constant companion: his security, a source of pride, his deliverer, and his provider.

For many immigrants to this new world, the trail west began around the port of New Castle in Delaware, and would lead to the counties of York and Lancaster in Pennsylvania. From there, westward expansion took the new arrivals into Virginia, and from there, down the Shenandoah Valley into North Carolina, Tennessee, and Kentucky.

Centers of gunsmithing expertise often formed around outposts that served as staging areas for settlers on their way down the Shenandoah Valley. The Pennsylvania towns of Lancaster and York became home to a significant population of German settlers: artisans who were highly skilled in many trades—including gunsmithing. Beginning about 1770, these remarkable craftsmen were busy developing what is recognized today as the Kentucky rifle.

Crockett's Rifles

As would any capable frontiersman, Crockett always had a long rifle close at hand. His rifles were often on his mind, which one can see from the many references in his autobiography. For example, Crockett writes:

> I continued in this down-spirited situation for a good long time, until one day I took my rifle and started a hunting. [*Narrative*, 57]

Or again on page 59:

> I employed my time pretty generally in giving information of it, as far as I could, until the day came; and I then offered to work for my old friend, the Quaker, two days, if he would let his bound boy go with me one to the reaping. He refused,

and reproved me pretty considerable roughly for my proposition; and said, if he was in my place he wouldn't go; that there would be a great deal of bad company there; and that I had been so good a boy, he would be sorry for me to get a bad name. But I knowed my promise to the Dutch girl, and I was resolved to fulfil it; so, I shouldered my rifle, and started by myself.

Crockett mentioned "my old friend, the Quaker." Quakers had little use for guns; they were staunchly opposed to military service and generally did not believe in either gambling or hunting for sport. David expressed great affection for his rifles, but they were a source of contention between him and his Quaker employer. Crockett's *Narrative* reflected that he would often avoid the issue around the Quaker, noting that he would slip out to attend shooting matches, saying, "I always tried, though, to keep it a secret from him" [*N*, 51].

Despite his willingness to make accommodation for Quaker sensibilities, Crockett enjoyed the camaraderie of shooting competitions. In his *Narrative*, Crockett wrote:

Just now I heard of a shooting-match in the neighbourhood, right between where I lived [Panther Spring] and my girl's house [Finley Gap]; and I determined to kill two birds with one stone, —to go to the shooting-match first, and then to see her. I therefore made the Quaker believe I was going to hunt for deer, as they were pretty plenty about in those parts; but, instead of hunting them, I went straight on to the shooting-match, where I joined in with a partner, and we put in several shots for the beef. I was mighty lucky, and when the match was over, I had won the whole beef. This was on a Saturday, and my success had put me in the finest humour in the world. So, I sold my part of the beef for five dollars in the real grit ... [*N*, 52]

The Crockett/McCuistion/Swann Rifle

As much as he loved his rifles and the competition of shooting matches, it wasn't unusual for Crockett to barter away a valued rifle for necessities he required, like a new horse. In one section of his *Narrative,* Crockett noted his growing impatience to strike out on his own. Looking to make his own way, he traded one of his rifles, along with three months of labor, for a "low-priced horse" with which he could begin farming [*N*, 64].

Insight into the comparative trading value of horses and rifles can be found in the estate listings of deceased individuals in Jefferson County at the time (Will Book #1 for the period 1796–1805), which contains appraisals for large numbers of both rifles and horses. This reference shows the average value of a horse at about $69, with a survey of rifle values showing an average of $14.62 each. A "low-priced horse" might be valued around $50. Doing some math to estimate the value of Crockett's rifle, one may estimate the value of three months of labor at about $6 to $7 per month, or about $20 total. It's reasonable to estimate that Crockett's rifle might have been valued at about $25, substantially more than the average rifle.

This April 1806 rifle/labor/horse exchange was contracted between David and Charles Canaday, his teacher and the married son of John Canaday, and was probably executed just prior to the issuance of Crockett's wedding license to Polly in early August 1806.[11]

Crockett would trade another rifle for necessities—which is how the Crockett/McCuistion/Swann rifle came to the attention of history. In 1811, Crockett was around age twenty-five and in the process of moving his family from Finley Gap in Jefferson County, Tennessee, to the Duck and Elk River country near today's Winchester, Tennessee. David owed a debt to neighbor James McCuistion, who ran a country store out of his farm just up the ridge on nearby Long Creek (today

---

11   Charles M. Canaday, *Canaday Family History*, Indianapolis, IN. Typewritten genealogy of the Canaday Family written prior to 1928. Copies furnished September 14,
1994 by Marilyn V. Harvey.

one mile north of the junction of Interstates 40 and 81). To satisfy this debt to McCuistion, David offered this rifle in partial payment to settle his debts prior to leaving Jefferson County.

The Crockett rifle traded to McCuistion weighed in at just over ten pounds. The 44" octagonal swamped barrel (wider at lock and barrel ends, tapering at the center for a balance of strength and weight) had seven rifling grooves in a barrel measuring .49 caliber. The stock displayed simple but elegant carving, a simplicity and elegance that was also reflected in the rifle's brass patch box.

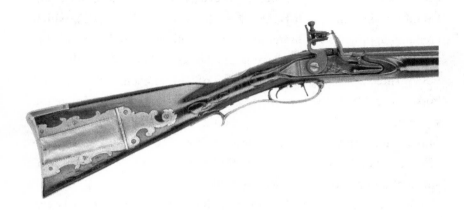

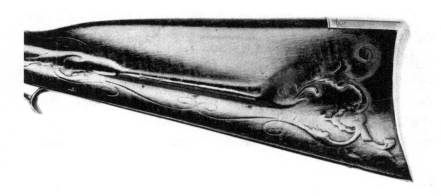

The Crockett rifle has remained in the McCuistion/Swann family since that day, though not without some legal wrangling over the years. After the sudden death of the rifle's owner, Samuel Scott McCuistion, in 1893, in which he died without a will, Judge Alexander Hynds of Dandridge, Tennessee, was tasked with settling McCuistion's estate. The file of McCuistion's estate settlement (found in the Jefferson County, Tennessee, Courthouse) contains a document dated January 25, 1893, and titled, "An Inventory of the personal property belonging to the estate of Maj. Saml. S. McCuistion, Decsd." This estate inventory shows personal items including:

> 1 old gold watch, and the Davy Crockett rifle gun.

A later document titled, "Sale list of the estate of S. S. McCuistion, D'csd held at his late house Feby 6, 1893," documents the presence of the Crockett rifle among McCuistion's estate goods, but notes:

> The Davy Crockett rifle gun was not offered at this sale, but the admst expects to sell same, maybe privately.

In the *Louisville* (Kentucky) *Courier-Journal* later in 1893, Judge Hynds recounts the story of Crockett in his article: "Davy Crockett. Something About the Famous Old Hero and His Rifle," where he writes:

> This gun was purchased by Mr. James McCuistion, Sr., a friend and neighbor to young Kennedy [McCuistion was a friend and neighbor of the Finleys, not Kennedy/Canaday], and it became an heirloom in the McCuistion family, the first owner [James McCuistion] leaving it to his son, the late Major Sam McCuistion, whose sudden death took place here recently. The rifle, which has never been out of the county except as an exhibit since Crockett parted with it in 1806, is beyond question the most valuable personal relic

of him in the state; indeed, this writer knows of no other so valuable. It is in a fine state of preservation; large bore, long barrel, flint lock, brass mounting, with the date 1792 scratched on the side-plate, while another has a crude Indian face in profile. The stock is fine curly maple, with a large grease pan at the butt.[12]

In settling McCuistion's estate, Judge Hynds made several attempts to sell the Crockett/McCuistion rifle. When the rifle was not sold, it was delivered to McCuistion's closest male heir, his nephew Sam Gwinn, who later left Dandridge with the rifle at an early age when he struck west for a job as a railroad agent in Goodwell, Oklahoma. Eugene Swann later saw the rifle in Goodwell in 1916 on a visit there.

In a 1989 article written by the late John Bivens in National Muzzle Loading Rifle Association's magazine *Muzzle Blasts,* his article "Crockett Redivivus: A Painstaking Recreation of Davy's First Rifle," says:

A rifle seemingly possessing every scrap of provenance needed to establish a particularly fine flintlock rifle as the former property of one Davy Crockett. ... One becomes jaundiced after encountering half a dozen "Boone" rifles which we've periodically been expected to genuflect before, as if they were a piece of the True Toenail. ... Here was a piece that most frontiersmen would have had to shuck out a half-year's wages to own. ... It is indeed fortunate that the McCuistions and their descendants had so carefully preserved a "paper chain" with the rifle, but each of them quite obviously recognized the importance of anything that had belonged to Crockett. ... It's a fine thing that an

---

12   Judge Alexander Hynds, "Davy Crockett. Something About the Famous Old Hero and His Rifle," *Louisville Courier Journal* (Monday morning, February 13, 1893): Page 7.

eighteenth-century rifle of exceptional quality, owned by one of America's best-known woodsmen, has survived for us to enjoy.[13]

Crockett was known to appreciate finely crafted rifles. Another long gun said to have been owned by Crockett while in Jefferson County, Tennessee, is credited to gunsmith Henry Bradford, who lived in the Long Creek neighborhood near the Finleys and McCuistions at the same time that David lived on his rented farm there. *Sketches of Prominent Tennesseans* (1888) noted that "Col. Henry Bradford was an excellent gunsmith, and he made the gun that Davy Crockett called his 'Long Bess.'"[14]

A later historical account in the *Chattanooga Times* noted that Henry Bradford:

> … came to Jefferson County about 1796. … He was many years a noted gunsmith in that region, and made more than 1,300 guns with his own hands. When in his eightieth year he made a fine gun and gave it to his son W. M. Bradford. He was also for many years a justice of the peace in Jefferson county. Tradition says that he performed the [1806] marriage ceremony of David Crockett and Polly Finley, and as a wedding present, gave Crockett an excellent rifle of his own make. Tradition also reports that Crockett prized this weapon highly, and that he carried and used it for many years.[15]

The McCuistion/Crockett rifle was on display in the Tennessee

---

13   John Bivens, "Crockett Redivivus: A Painstaking Recreation of Davy's First Rifle," *Muzzle Blasts*, Vol. 50, no. 5 (January 1989): 4.

14   Wm. S. Speer, *Sketches of Prominent Tennesseans* (Nashville: A. B. Tavel, 1888), 132.

15   Charles W. Lusk, *Chattanooga Times* (October 6, 1942): 16.

State Museum in Nashville from 1982 to 1995, then moved to the Museum of East Tennessee History in Knoxville, where it resides today. This is a classic Kentucky rifle, made in the finest traditions of the Pennsylvania masters. To commemorate the two hundredth birthday of Crockett in 1986, this rifle was prominently featured in a joint exhibition at the National Portrait Gallery of the Smithsonian Institution, Washington, DC, and the Tennessee State Museum in Nashville. This Crockett rifle was photographed for the publication, *Davy Crockett: Gentleman from the Cane*, which accompanied the exhibition.

The McCuistion/Crockett rifle is fully stocked in curly maple, brass-mounted, and crafted during the Golden Age of that artform. It would have been immediately recognized in Crockett's time for its superior appearance and construction. The late George Shumway, a preeminent authority on Pennsylvania-made Kentucky rifles, writing for *Muzzle Blasts* magazine in 1980, said:

> It is a beautifully made, relief-carved piece from the late eighteenth century. … Without a doubt it is a grand old rifle, made in the best traditions of Pennsylvania gunsmithing at the beginning of the Golden Age of rifle making [ca. 1780–1790]. … My hypothesis will be that this rifle was made in York County [Pennsylvania], until reason to believe otherwise comes along.[16]

Much has been made of Crockett's name for his rifle: *Betsey* (or *Betsy*). Crockett's biography contains no references to *Betsy*, but there is good reason to believe that David probably did refer to many of his firearms as *Betsy*. The name appears in the earlier Crockett biography *Sketches,* which contains at least ten references to his rifle as *Betsey*

---

16   George Shumway, "Long Rifles of Note," *Muzzle Blasts*, (October 1980): 16–18.

or *old Betsy*.[17] The Disney productions of the 1950s called attention to that name used in the *Sketches* biography.

Yet, it was quite common at the time to name a rifle for a wife, sweetheart, sister, or other female in the frontiersman's life. For example, Robert Young's rifle "Sweet Lips" was named for his wife, and was used to kill British Col. Ferguson. David's oldest sister, Elizabeth "Betsy" Crockett, who was the first to recognize him after his return from the three-year trip to Virginia, was probably his favorite sister and might have been the namesake for his rifles. Born about 1788, Betsy later married a Quaker, Yarnell Reese, on November 25, 1805. She apparently kept up with David throughout his life, as David later secured land for Betsy and Yarnell in Gibson County, Tennessee, where they are listed in the Gibson County Census of 1850.

---

17   Clarke, *Sketches*, 66, 67, 69, 84, 91, 102, 106, 119, 122, 144.

CHAPTER 2:

Crockett Ancestors in Pennsylvania, Virginia, and North Carolina

In his *Narrative*, David Crockett wrote:

> My father's name was John Crockett, and he was of Irish descent. He was either born in Ireland or on a passage from that country to America across the Atlantic. He was by profession a farmer, and spent the early part of his life in the state of Pennsylvania. The name of my mother was Rebecca Hawkins. She was an American woman, born in the state of Maryland, between York [Pennsylvania] and Baltimore. [*N*, 14]

Regarding the reliability of Davy's accounts of his early family history, University of Tennessee professor Dr. Stanley Folmsbee indicated that he believed it was Crockett's grandfather David, and not his father, John, who was born in Ireland or during the ocean passage.[18]

---

18   *Narrative*, 14.

Yet, John Crockett's likely birth year of 1750 would seem to support David's account of his father's history.

Nevertheless, as part of the great settler migration arriving from Northern Ireland, the Crocketts were seasoned veterans of hostile environments and were in the vanguard of Europeans seeking a new home and new opportunities in America. After the Crockett ancestors made the passage from Ireland to New York in the early 1700s, the family would soon move to Pennsylvania. Variations of the Crockett name would appear in 1732 issues of the *Philadelphia Gazette* (a newspaper printed by Benjamin Franklin). For example:

> "Philadelphia, Sept. 18. This day arrived here Capt. Crokat with 250 Dutch Passengers, in 7 weeks from England, Ship Johnson Gally, David Crokat, from Deal." A David Crockett was mentioned in October 25 and November 23 issues of the paper, both noting: "David Crockatt, to South Carolina."

It is unknown if there is any connection with this Captain Crokat and the family of David Crockett, but it is worth mentioning for future study.

Pennsylvania was but one stop on a long and arduous journey for the Crockett family, then south into the part of northern Virginia that is known today as West Virginia. We know that by 1748, Crockett's grandparents David and Elizabeth Crockett were located in the very northernmost part of Frederick County, Virginia, "4 miles from Watkins Ferry lying on both sides of the Wagon Road" just over the Pennsylvania line.[19] We also know that they had relocated to Tryon (later Lincoln County), North Carolina, before 1771 and were in East Tennessee by July 1776.

The name of Crockett appeared with some regularity in legal documents in Pennsylvania and the Virginias. A David Crockett,

---

19   Frederick County, Va., Deed Bk H, 571 and 666. Also Kathryn Jones, *Crockett Cousins* (self-published, 1984), 4.

presumably Davy's grandfather, was witness to a lease between Morgan Bryan (grandfather of Rebecca Bryan Boone, wife of Daniel Boone) and Roger Turner in Frederick County, Virginia, in January 1743.[20] Morgan Bryan had come to Virginia about 1730 and brought settlers from Pennsylvania with him. Crockett's name appearing on a legal document such as a lease suggests that he knew and associated with the Boone family. John Crockett did live in Pennsylvania, as Davy states, so he would have to have been at least 38 years old when Davy was born (if grandfather David Crockett's family were living in Virginia by 1748). The family lived and moved along the borders of Pennsylvania, Virginia, and today's West Virginia, which makes it difficult to determine exactly when they left Pennsylvania and moved into Northern Virginia.

David's grandfather David (ca. 1725–1777)[21] and grandmother Elizabeth Crockett were some of the early settlers of the area around Winchester, Virginia. The Crockett family lived for a time in Nollville, Virginia (now West Virginia), twenty miles north of Winchester, and later in Berryville, twenty miles south. David Crockett was listed among the tithables (or "taxpayers") of this county in 1748.[22]

When it came to breaking new trails in dangerous country, grandfather David and his sons demonstrated their willingness to be vigorous and take chances in exchange for expanding their horizons and opportunities. The sons of David and Elizabeth Crockett were listed as William (born ca. 1745–1748), Robert, John (Davy's father), David Jr., Joseph, James, and Alexander. Davy's uncle Robert Crockett

---

20   Sullivan County #2165, November 8, 1779, William Crockett for Alexander & James Crockett orphans of David Crockett deceased, 400 acres in Sullivan Co on N side of Holston River and on head waters of Back Creek, including said Crockett deceased's improvement; warrant issued Oct. 13, 1780 by Landon Carter, 400 acres surveyed January 24, 1788, for "Thomas Randen" (sic Rankin) by Arthur Moore; 400 acres entered by William Crocket on entry taker's report; (for grant see file #1204 in Greene Co; MARS 12.14.6.1204).

21   Jones, Crockett Cousins, 2.

22   Frederick County Virginia, Order Book 2, 3 August 1748, 456.

filed for a Revolutionary War Pension in 1833 and stated that he was born August 13, 1755, in Berryville, Virginia.[23] It seems likely that there would have been daughters in this family, but records of them are absent. Davy's eldest uncle William appears in court records in 1760 (William would have been a teenager), where he was noted as the recipient of some kind of legal judgment in favor of himself and his younger brother James. In a document from Chester County, Pennsylvania, titled: "No. 117, January Term of 1760, to the Sheriff of Cumberland County, James Crockett and William Crockett," the brothers were noted as having been awarded "40 pounds, seventy-three shillings and 3 pence lawful money of Pennsylvania from John Brownlee, Sr and John Brownlee, Jr of West Collen Township, Chester County, Pennsylvania." The document was witnessed by a John Armstrong, Esquire, at the town of Carlisle, Pennsylvania.

It appears that the David Crockett family left Frederick County, Virginia, around the middle of 1768. The Crocketts sold 352 acres of land to Robert Watt, "within four miles of Watkins Ferry, it being a patent granted to a certain Jonas Hedges and his wife Elizabeth, bearing a date of 7th of Sept. 1756."[24] It is believed that Jonas and Elizabeth Hedges may have been Elizabeth Crockett's parents (it was common for daughters to have their mother's name). As there is no record of David Crockett's purchase of the 352 acres, he may have been selling a parcel that belonged to his father-in-law.[25] One source says that Davy's father, John, was at one time at Point Pleasant, Virginia.[26]

David says in his *Narrative* that: "My father, as I have understood, lived in Lincoln County, in the state of North Carolina" [*N*, 15]. There are numerous records of Crocketts in Lincoln County, North Carolina, a jurisdiction that absorbed the old Tryon County (now extinct).

---

23   Folmsbee/Shackford, Annotated *Narrative*, 14, note 3.

24   Frederick County Virginia, Book H, 666.

25   Jones, *Crockett Cousins*, 4.

26   Lula P. Givens, *Christiansburg, Montgomery County, Virginia, in The Heart of the Alleghenies* (Pulaski, VA: Edmonds Printing, Inc., 1981), 37.

The sons of David and Elizabeth Crockett about whom the least is known are David, Jr. and Alexander (Davy Crockett's uncles). It is known that a David, *Jr.* and *Sr.* witnessed a deed in Tryon County, North Carolina, in 1771.[27] It is also known that two David Crocketts signed (one after the other) the Washington County, Tennessee, Petition to Virginia in November 1777.

This David Crockett, Jr. appears to have taken off in a different direction from William and John soon after their arrival in what is today northeast Tennessee, as he does not appear in the records of the counties of upper East Tennessee after these early entries.

William Crockett was clearly active in other land trading. On January 11, 1785, an Isaac Kimbal of Lincoln County sold land on Kings Creek to a William Crockett, a transaction that was witnessed by John and Sarah Wilson. A William Crockett also owned another tract that had been previously owned by James Patterson and David Elder. By some accounts, one of David's brothers may have been named Patterson Crockett[28] and one of David's first cousins married the daughter of a David Elder in Jefferson County, Tennessee.[29]

Although many of the Ulster-Scots immigrants were poor, their culture and Presbyterian religion put a high value on education. A sizable number of these immigrants could read and write. The Carter's Valley Petition to *The Provincial Council of North Carolina* written in 1776 was signed by 116 mostly Ulster-Scots residents of what was to become Tennessee. David and William Crockett signed the Washington District petition to the State of North Carolina in 1776. Again in 1777, two David Crocketts, along with John and William Crockett, signed the Carter's Valley petitions to Virginia.

Of those 116 signatories, fully 114 of them signed their names, leaving only two unlettered signers who were able only to make their

---

27   Jones, *Crockett Cousins*, 8. Tryon Co, NC: Samuel Coburn sells to John Delozier land on October 6, 1767, witnessed by David Crockett, Jr. and David Crockett, Sr.

28   Jones, *Crockett Cousins*, 23.

29   Jones, *Crockett Cousins*, 115.

"mark" or an "X" on the petition. For this time in history, not many remote frontier regions could boast such a high number of residents who could write.

CHAPTER 3:

The Crocketts Arrive in East Tennessee

During the year of 1776, John Crockett (ca. 1753–1834), with his father, David, his mother, Elizabeth, and brothers William, Robert, David Jr., Joseph, James, and probably Alexander, left Lincoln County, North Carolina, for East Tennessee. It is likely that the Crocketts followed the mountain trail blazed by Daniel Boone (who had lived on Beaver Creek, near King's Creek around 1767 to 1768). The Crockett clan settled near Rogersville, Tennessee. Brothers William, Robert, David Jr., and Joseph established separate households near their parents.[30]

At this time, the land in the Watauga settlement in northeast Tennessee (including Washington, Sullivan, and Hawkins Counties) was thought to be in Virginia. Sometimes referred to as the "Republic of Watauga," this community along the Watauga River in what is today Elizabethton, Tennessee, was a semi-autonomous government founded in 1772 by frontier settlers. Although it endured for only a few years, the Watauga Association was a precursor for what later developed into the state of Tennessee. The boundaries between Virginia and North Carolina had not been adequately surveyed that far west at

---

30   A Narrative of the Life of David Crockett of the State of Tennessee.

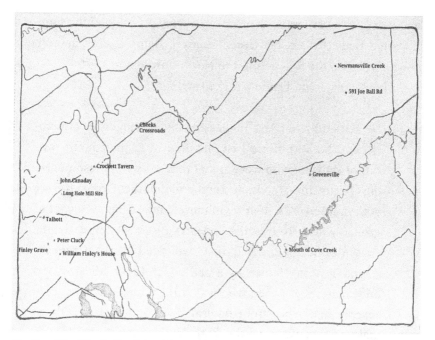

Caption: The King's Creek land in North Carolina, originally Tryon County.

the time. The surging tide of settlers was moving west faster than the states could survey their boundary lines to keep up with them. By the time Tennessee was established as a state in 1796, the borders were sorted out, surveyed, and codified.

There is no doubt that the Crocketts were one of the very first settler families to come to this rugged, dangerous, and resource-rich land known then as *Tennassee*. David Crockett, Sr. and his eldest son William signed the Washington District Petition to North Carolina on July 5, 1776, requesting that the Watauga community be annexed into North Carolina. Others who signed this petition (who have established or probable connections to the Crockett family) included Jacob Brown; Gideon, Daniel, Groves, and Shadrach Morris; Matthew Hawkins; Valentine and Robert Sevier; Henry Siler; William Dod; Charles and Joseph McCartney; and five members of the Cox family. A Carter's Valley petition was signed in 1776 and 1777 by Davy's father, John, and uncles William and David Crockett. Some of the other families who were early settlers in the Watauga country included the families of Carter, Bean, Robertson, Greer, Sherrell, Bates, Easley, and others who also signed the first petition to North Carolina in 1776.

Of his father, John, David Crockett wrote:

> He settled there [East Tennessee] under dangerous circum-stances, both to himself and his family, as the country was full of Indians, who were at that time very troublesome. By the Creeks, my grandfather and grandmother Crockett were both murdered, in their own house, and on the very spot of ground where Rogersville, in Hawkins County, now stands. At the same time, the Indians wounded Joseph Crockett, a brother to my father, by a ball which broke his arm; and took James a prisoner, who was still a younger brother than Joseph, and who, from natural defects, was less able to make his escape, as he was both deaf and dumb. [*N*, 15–16]

After David and Elizabeth Crockett were killed in this Indian attack, which included both Creeks and Cherokee, their eldest sons William and Robert Crockett were named executors of the family's estate. John Coulter and John Lowery were security for them as recorded in the Washington County, Virginia, court minutes for the August term of 1778. This date supports the likely year of the attack being around 1777. Family records of Charles Canaday, a Quaker with whom Davy lived for several years, reported that small children in the Crockett household were also killed in the attack.[31] The graves of David and Elizabeth Crockett can be viewed today in the Rogers Cemetery, sur-rounded by a low stone wall in the town of Rogersville, Tennessee, on the property where they died.[32]

After the deaths of David and Elizabeth Crockett, a land grant in their estate was sold for the benefit of the orphaned Crockett children.

---

31   Canaday, *Canaday Family History*.

32   Jefferson County Will Book 2, April 3, 1818, 237.

This parcel was located about thirty miles southwest of Rogersville, and was sold to Thomas Rankin, as follows:

> I do assign overall our right and title of this, within Warrant, unto Thomas Rankin. Witness by hand this 1st Day of June 1788: William Crockett, Alexander Crockett, James Crockett

> Surveyed for Thomas Rankin, 400 acres of land by virtue of North Carolina Land Office, Warrant No 2165 and dated Nov 8 1779, lying and being in Greene County on the waters of Long Creek including the Improvement said Rankin now lives on. Viz begin at a Black Oak ... Jan 24, 1788

> Arthur Moore A.S.Q.G.B.
> John Cunningham and Arthur Moore C B [survey chain bearers]

The former Crockett homestead, sold to Thomas Rankin to benefit the orphaned Crockett children, became known as the "Duffield Rankin Home" (pictured nearby; photo courtesy of Elda McMurray, August 3, 1979). The home sat along Dumplin Valley Road near Dandridge, Tennessee. There is little doubt that young Davy Crockett spent much of his time in this house.

It is interesting to note that the land surveyed for Rankin (forty miles from Rogersville in what is today Jefferson County) would be only a ten-minute walk from where Davy would have his first home and where his first children were born.

Not long after, another land warrant was executed by David's uncle William Crockett in the names of William's younger brothers, Alexander and James Crockett. The warrant read:

> North Carolina, Washington County, November 8, 1779, [Warrant] No 2165, To the Surveyor of Sullivan County,

Greetings. You are hereby Required to Measure and lay off A warrant to Law, four hundred acres of Land Entered by William Crockett for Alexander and James Crockett, Orphans of David Crockett, Decesd [deceased] on the waters of the Holston on the head Waters of Back Creek, including said Crockett Decesd Improvement, Given under my hand at office the day the 7 Oct 1780. [signed] Landon Carter E. Q. 241

This land warrant suggests that, as the eldest brother, William may have served in a guardian capacity to his younger siblings after the 1777 death of their parents. William clearly handled the sale of land owned by their late father as an inheritance to minor orphaned sons Alexander and James. It seems odd, but at that time, parent-less sons or daughters younger than twenty-one years of age must have been considered orphans.

The land warrant on behalf of orphans Alexander and James was likely filed *in absentia* for James, since he had been taken prisoner in the Indian attack that killed his parents. James Crockett (Davy's uncle) remained in Indian captivity for the next nineteen years. While it is difficult to imagine what James Crockett must have endured during his nineteen years of living among the Creeks, it is testimony to the toughness of these early settlers that James Crockett went on to live for many years after his return from captivity. In fact, James Crockett later took trips with various groups of neighbors, trying to find a silver mine he says the Cherokee had shown him while he was a captive.

Sometime after the deaths of David and Elizabeth, their son John located about three miles south of Rogersville and likely married Rebecca Hawkins sometime between 1777 and 1780. Rebecca Hawkins, Davy's mother, was likely the daughter of Nathan Hawkins (the son of Rebecca Hawkins and the grandson of Matthew Hawkins and Mary Parrish of Baltimore County, Maryland) and Ruth Cole Hawkins,[33] who were married February 14, 1744, in a ceremony recorded at St. Paul's Church, Baltimore. According to David, his mother, Rebecca, had been born between Baltimore and York, Pennsylvania.[34]

According to one account, the names of a sister and brother named Rebecca and Joseph Hawkins were found in records of St. John's P. E. Church at Old Joppa on the Gunpowder River, in what is now in Harford County, Maryland.[35] While these two Hawkins siblings were listed with birth dates in the late 1720s, making them a generation too old to be David's mother and uncle, they were from the area of Maryland between Baltimore and York, Pennsylvania, and thus might be connected to Rebecca Hawkins's family.

Two of Rebecca's brothers are believed to have been Aaron and Joseph. Joseph Hawkins lived near Davy's family when they lived in Greene County north of Greeneville. Rebecca's father, Nathan, died between 1781 and 1783, and his estate records are listed in Sullivan County, Tennessee.

---

33   Lusk, *Chattanooga Times* (October 6, 1942): 16.

34   A Narrative of the Life of David Crockett of the State of Tennessee.

35   Robert Torrence and Robert L. Whittenburg, *Colonel "Davy" Crockett. A Geneaology* (Washington, DC: Homer Fagan, 1956), 3–4.

No record of the marriage of John and Rebecca Hawkins Crockett has been found to date, but in 1783, John and Rebecca Hawkins Crockett received a land grant in Sullivan County in northeast Tennessee. While they kept the land until 1787, the Crocketts moved from the Rogersville area to land owned by Colonel George Gillespie, across the river from Fort Lee where Strong Springs empties into the Nolichucky River (now part of the David Crockett State Park).

Colonel Gillespie had obtained this land by North Carolina Grant #98, entered May 25, 1778. He had likely procured a title or lease from Jacob Brown, the first White man to trade in land with the Cherokees in what has become known as Brown's Purchase. He was an itinerant merchant from South Carolina who began trading with the Cherokees at an early date and likely acquired the land through direct negotiation with the Cherokees (rather than through a US government land office).

Fort Lee offered the safety of living near a frontier garrison, which may have influenced John's decision to move the family there after the vulnerability he witnessed in the Cherokee attack that killed his parents. It was here that young Davy Crockett was born at Limestone on August 17, 1786.

According to a Knoxville newspaper article, ca. 1900–1910, the site of David's birth was:

> Just across the river to the south were the Old Fields, once the playgrounds of the Cherokees, … Hard by were yet the remains of the home of Captain Thomas Gillespie. This home was one of the markers for the line between the two counties as laid off in 1783.

> On a hill above stood an old fort [Fort Lee] in 1777, Commanded by General Joseph Martin, then a lieutenant, but later on promoted to high position. This fort was shelter to the Watauga settlement. In the previous year, old Abraham had led his Cherokees up the south side of the river, crossed at Brown's Station, and approached the Watauga fort by

way of the Big Cherokee creek, thus forcing the garrison at the mouth of the Big Limestone to retreat.

One huge double log house stood on the high ground east of the fort of the Limestone [the Earnest Fort House still standing at this writing], and portholes were pointed as having been used against the Indians. Just north of this was an equally old building with like history. It was beside the dam that had a mill below it on the west side of the road, the water coming from the Limestone Creek. All were then large oaks and many cedars on the higher ground, while between there and Fullen's Depot the timber was scrub oak in part with an occasional large tree.

The ford across the Big Limestone was the sleekest thing I ever saw. The floor of the ford was of large smooth limestone rock covered with a slime that looked innocent but spelled disaster to man or beast who waded it. Feet up and head down was the rule. One old gentleman declared that the elders used to relate how John Sevier when fording it had his horse slip and throw him into the water. When the mill was running and the water passed into the mill race above the ford, it was not so bad, ... There must have been some gypsum deposit above that impregnated water. Middleton's fall is simple.[36]

The information in the article is corroborated by Speer in *Sketches of Prominent Tennesseans*:

The boundaries of Brown's settlement, on the west, extended down the Nolichucky, below the mouth of Big Limestone Creek, and that neighborhood being the weakest and first

---

36   Bivens, "Crockett Redivivus," *Muzzle Blasts*, 4.

exposed, a fort was built, at Gillespie's, near the river, and a garrison was stationed in it.[37]

Fort Lee was built around 1775 to 1776 at the mouth of Big Limestone Creek, just prior to the massacre of Davy's grandparents. While settlers were often in conflict with the Indian tribes, tenuous alliance between the two sometimes proved lifesaving for White settlers. It was around July 1776 when Old Abraham of Chilhowee and the dreaded Cherokee Chief Dragging Canoe led a war party against Fort Lee and Watauga Fort.[38]

The female Cherokee Chief Nancy Ward was one ally who was held in high regard by the White families who were moving into Cherokee lands. Her warnings to the Watauga settlers, including David's father and mother, allowed the families to move back to the protection of the forts in advance of war parties being led by Chief Dragging Canoe. Her advance notice of impending attack undoubtedly saved the lives of many families who were vulnerable to attack. Prior to his birth, David's parents were one of these families of upper East Tennessee, who revered Chief Nancy Ward and owed her their lives. As recounted by writer Melissa Boher:

> Four white traders, led by Isaac Thomas, slipped out of Chota sometime during the day or night of July 8, 1776, carrying Chief Nancy Ward's message of warning to the Overmountain settlements. They reached Fort Lee (Limestone, Tennessee) July 11, ten days before Old Abram's attack on Fort Watauga and nine days before Dragging Canoe's battle at Island Flats (Kingsport, Tennessee). The warning of an imminent Indian attack on the Holston, Watauga, and Nolichucky people was not a surprise. Such a move had been anticipated for some time, and special efforts had been made to ready the forts

---

37   Speer, *Sketches of Prominent Tennesseans*, 132.

38   Tennessee During the Revolutionary War by Samuel Cole Williams

and stockades for the expected onslaught. The timely warning did give women and children ample time to reach the nearest fort for protection.

Any speculation about Nancy Ward's reasons for sending the warning message to the whites is pure conjecture. However, recorded words, actions, and written documents regarding her later years, reveal some clues to her purposes and thinking. One of Nancy's most common sayings was, "The white men are our brothers, the same house shelters us, and the same sky covers us all." Her cry was ALL FOR PEACE.[39]

The settlers in the Fort Lee area received word from the peacemaker Cherokee Chief Nancy Ward that hostile Cherokees were on their way to attack. The settlers and garrison immediately fled to the better-fortified Watauga Fort, leaving everything behind at Fort Lee. The advancing Cherokees destroyed the fort, crops, and the belongings of these families. While Fort Lee was lost, the settlers successfully defended Fort Watauga from the attack with the reinforcements from Gillespie's.

David's father, John, demonstrated his ability to write his name, and further to create legal documents when he served as a magistrate of the failed State of Franklin, then comprising a dozen counties on the eastern edge of Tennessee. For example, in an order to Capt. John Tadlock, drawn to Daniel Kennedy, Clerk of the Court, State of Franklin, dated May 26, 1787, John Crockett wrote:

---

39   Melissa Boher, *Glory, Passion, and Principle: The story of eight remarkable women at the core of the American Revolution* (New York: Atria Books, 2003).

Sir: Be pleased to Pay the Bearer Daniel Kennedy One/
Pound Franklin money and You will Oblige—Yours xc

jc John Crocket [40]

Capt. John Tadlock.[41]

While John Crockett was known for his hard luck and financial
troubles, his role as a magistrate and constable in the State of Franklin
and Greene County demonstrated that he may well have been more
capable and educated than his lack of success in life would indicate.
The Tadlock note establishes that John Crockett had a good command
of language, an understanding of legal form and terminology, and
could write passably. While his financial misfortunes in land speculation and the Cove Creek mill disaster (perhaps complicated by alco-
holism), may have derailed a once-promising career as a respected
member of the local community, his appointment as a magistrate suggested that John Crockett had at least earned a degree of respect in
early Greene County (formed in April 1783 from parts of Washington
County), where John and his brothers William and Robert were also
elected constables.[42]

John Crockett's ability to write allowed him to participate in civic
affairs, such as signing onto the formal Petition of Inhabitants of
the Western Country (dated December 1787), requesting the formation of the State of Franklin. Numerous other men associated with
the Crocketts signed this petition, including John Corson [Carson];
David Rankin; Henry Earnest; James Stinson; Thomas Millikin;
John Galbreath; Stephen Strong; John Noman [Newman]; Reuben,

---

40   The abbreviation *jc* before the signature presumably meant *Justice of the Court*.

41   L. W. Reynolds, "The Pioneer Crockett Family of Tennessee," *Daughters of the
      American Revolution Magazine* LV, (April 1921): 188. [Shackford's Annotated
      Narrative, unpublished, contains the note p. 178, FN #2].

42   Clarke, *Sketches*, p. 1, 66, 67, 69, 84, 91, 102, 106, 122.

Dalton, and Simon Riggs; Miller Dogget; Joseph Hamilton; Thomas, Elias, and Nathaniel Witt; Nicholas Hayes; Alexander Lowery; John Spurgin; Samuel and Jacob Cox; Joseph Yancey; Andrew Jackson; and Gilbert Christian.[43]

As a magistrate, John Crockett may have presided at the issuance of Andrew Jackson's first law license in 1794, according to Shackford.[44] This could have been true, in that he had official duties in Greene County and the State of Franklin at a time when Andrew Jackson was actively practicing law in the area. It was customary for newly arrived lawyers to appear in front of the magistrate to present their qualification as an attorney, and to receive a license from the local governing body.

David makes no mention of an interaction between his father, John, and Andrew Jackson, a man who would later become Davy's nemesis. Because of Davy's tendency in his *Narrative* to lash out at Jackson, it's likely that if he knew his father had interacted with Jackson, he would have mentioned it in his biography. The absence of this mention suggests Crockett may not have known that Jackson presented himself in John Crockett's court. The early Tennessee frontier was a small place in terms of the number of people who occupied it, if not in the number of people who made their way across it. The small population made the likelihood of individual interactions much higher than if the region had been crowded with roads, towns, and higher populations.

David would later show his ambition to learn to read and write and, like his father, became a magistrate as he began his rise in politics. David would demonstrate that he could sign his own name by age nineteen, as evidenced by his signature on the license to marry Polly Finley dated August 12, 1806.[45]

---

43   Petition of Inhabitants of the Western Country for the State of Franklin, December 1787.

44   Shackford, *David Crockett: The Man and the Legend*, 6.

45   David Crockett to Polly Finley, Marriage Bond, Jefferson County Courthouse, Dandridge, Tennessee, dated August 6, 1806.

David's and his father's pursuit of literacy may owe some credit to the Ulster-Scots Presbyterian value placed upon education. Early Greene County was populated by a mix of mainly Ulster-Scots, English, Welsh, and Germans (or "Dutch" as David referred to them). Greene County seemed to attract a greater German population than the surrounding counties. Names such as Meyers, Stonecypher, Earnest, Bull, Broyles, Coffman, Humberd, Heng, Huff, Harr, Hiss, Fien, and Bean were some of the Germanic family names of settlers who arrived early and might have known the Crocketts.

David states in his *Narrative* that he was born on August 17, 1786, "at the mouth of Limestone, on the Nola-chucky river," and that he was born the sixth child of John and Rebecca, among his five brothers and three sisters.[46] At the time of his birth, the state of North Carolina and the short-lived State of Franklin contested the political status of the area that would soon become the state of Tennessee. David could later make the argument that he was born in three states at the same time—the states of North Carolina, Franklin, and Tennessee. The supposed site of the cabin in which David was born is designated today by a limestone marker placed there in 1889. According to one account: "In the memory of the oldest inhabitant, a stone chimney once stood, marking the site ..."[47]

The John and Rebecca Hawkins Crockett family consisted of nine children, including in order: daughter Ruth, William (married February 3, 1803, to Rebecca Elliott [b. 1786], and died October 23, 1854, in Shelby County, Illinois). Aaron was born March 7, 1782, and died September 25, 1804, and was married to Nancy, born April 14, 1781, in Maryland. Fourth child Nathan grew up to marry a girl named Margaret. Brother Patterson, born around 1784, married Nancy Gray in Christian County, Kentucky, on March 21, 1809, and died in 1834 in Gibson County, Tennessee. David himself, as the sixth child, was born August 17, 1786, followed by brother John, who was born

---

46   *Narrative*, 16–17.

47   Reynolds, "Pioneer Crockett Family," 188.

around 1787 and married Sally Ann Thomas on October 24, 1812, at Cheek's Crossroads.

David's brother John Crockett served in the War of 1812 in the 4th Regiment East Tennessee Militia under Colonel Samuel Bayless from November 1814 to May 1815. Their Jefferson County unit was under the command of Captain James Churchman, and included company members James Corbet, James Finley, John Crockett, John Churchman, Bradley Bettis, David Ashemore, Joel Cowan, Gaberial Lewis, Tidance Lane, James Walker, Gabriel Lewis, John H. Edgar, Jacob Denton, and Richard Grison [Grisham]. Davy's brother John Crockett died in 1841. Crockett's sister Elizabeth (or Betsy) was born around 1788 and married Yarnell Reese on November 25, 1805. Yarnell was the son of Thomas and Hannah Williams Reese, documented as Quakers living in Guilford, North Carolina, in 1774. David's youngest sibling was sister Rebecca, born around 1796 and who married John Foster of Lawrence County, Tennessee, on June 9, 1819.

In his *Narrative*, Davy recounts his earliest memories, "before he had ever worn any breeches." He tells one story of a potentially disastrous canoe incident. His four elder brothers and a fifteen-year-old boy named Campbell had gotten into a canoe and were drifting down the Nolichucky River toward a dangerous waterfall. The incident was supposed to have taken place at the location of David's birth in Greene County at the mouth of Limestone Creek:

> My four elder brothers, and a well-grown boy of about fifteen years old by the name of Campbell, and myself, were all playing on the river's side; when all of the rest of them got into my father's canoe, and put out to amuse themselves on the water, leaving me on the shore alone.

> Just a little distance below them, there was a fall in the river, which went slap-right straight down. My brothers, though they were little fellows, had been used to paddling the canoe, and could have carried it safely anywhere about

there; but this fellow Campbell wouldn't let them have the paddle, but, fool like, undertook to manage it himself … in a short time, here they were all going, straight forward, stern foremost, right plump to the falls; and if they had only had a fair shake, they would have gone over slick as a whistle. It was'ent this, though, that scared me; for I was so infernal mad that they had left me on the shore, that I had as soon have seen them all go over the falls a bit, as any other way … their danger was seen by a man by the name of Kendall, … This man Kendall was working in a field on the bank and knowing there was no time to lose, he started full tilt, and here he come like a cane break afire; and as he ran, he threw off his coat, and then his jacket, and then his shirt, for I know that when he got to the water he had nothing on but his breeches. But seeing him in such a hurry, and tearing off his clothes as he went, I had no doubt that the devil or something else was after him and close on to him, too as he was running within an inch of his life. This alarmed me and I screamed out like a young painter. But Kendall didn't stop for this. He went ahead with all his might. When he came to the water he plunged in, and where it was too deep to wade he would swim, and where it was shallow enough he went bolting on; and by such exertion as I never saw at any other time in my life, he reached the canoe, when it was within twenty or thirty feet of the falls … he hung on to the canoe, till he got it stop'd, and then draw'd it out of danger. When they got out, I found the boys were more scared than I had been, and the only thing that comforted me was, the belief that it was a punishment on them for leaving me on shore.[48]

This account from his autobiographical *Narrative* demonstrates Crockett's skill as a storyteller, proving to be meticulous in his

---

48   *Narrative*, 18–20.

attention to the details of his reminiscences. The reader can still go to the actual place described in Crockett's account and see the topography as he described it in his *Narrative*.

However, scholars Folmsbee and Shackford both doubted the credibility of this early incident. Folmsbee, on page 19 of the Annotated Edition of the *Narrative,* speculated that the story contained information that is evidence of material "fabricated" to make a political statement:

There are many names, which cannot be identified, and others are purposely fabricated. For instance, "a man by the name of Kendall" is probably fictitious, created to take a dig at Jackson; Amos Kendall was one of Jackson's confidential circle of friends as well as postmaster general.[49]

Despite Folmsbee's claim, it appears that the incident happened just as David tells it, including the names. One can still go today to the Crockett birthplace and see the spot in the river where the potentially tragic canoe incident took place. About two or three hundred yards downstream from the stone marker designating Crockett's birthplace, one finds a shoal on the Nolichucky River. At the bottom of the swift water is a turbulent sheer drop of perhaps five feet, which extends all the way across the river. At this point, the river makes a sharp bend to the left (southwest) against a massive limestone rock wall.

This waterfall is also documented in old deeds. When George H. Gillespie sold the birthplace property to Samuel Stonecypher in 1824, the deed refers to the property as "near the big falls."[50] A deed to the same tract of property in 1860 references "near Gelaspies Falls."[51] These natural falls would be a formidable obstacle to the most intrepid canoe expert, to say nothing of a canoe full of inexperienced children with one paddle between them.

The lands across the river from the Gillespie property were a part

---

49   Crockett, *Narrative* (Annotations by Shackford and Folmsbee), 19.

50   Greene County Deed Book 13, 308.

51   Hiram Remine to Elizabeth Falls, Greene County Deed Book 31, 344.

of the Elmwood Farm of Henry Earnest, who had purchased the land from Amos Bird in 1777. There he built a three-story log blockhouse in 1784 on the banks of the Nolichucky.[52] The Greene County will of Ephraim Broyles dated 19 March 1828, mentions a daughter Eve, whose husband was a George Kindle [Kendall], and executors of his estate Col. Henry Earnest (Jr.) and Joseph Earnest.

George Kindle witnessed two deeds for property on nearby Little Limestone Creek.[53] A deed was issued from James Scott to George Kindle and Martin Sidnor, dated February 24, 1794, for one hundred acres on the south fork of Little Limestone Creek, adjoining Jonathan Bird, Aaron Lewis, Moses Brooks, and Walter Car. A William Kindle is listed as a soldier of the Kings Mountain Battle.[54]

The case for George Kindle as the rescuer is strong. David said the man's name was Kendall, which is pronounced the same as Kindle. He has a traceable connection with the Earnest family directly across the Nolichucky and he was in the neighborhood at the time David says the incident occurred.

As for the Campbell youth, there is no direct evidence of who he was specifically, but there is evidence of a Campbell family in the area at the time. In North Carolina land grants in Tennessee, there are four Washington County grants to an Alexander Campbell, located very close to this spot. The Campbell land grants were substantial: in 1782, a grant for 224 acres on "the east side of Big Limestone Creek";[55] 100 acres on "both sides of great Limestone Creek";[56] and 207 acres "on

---

52   Greene County History Book Committee, *Historic Greene County, Tennessee and Its Peoples: 1783–1992* (Don Mills, 1992), 94.

53   Washington Co Deeds Beard to Bottles, 24–25, Bullers Branch of Little Limestone Creek, October 26, 1790, and Brown to Brown, 192, on Little Limestone Creek, August 11, 1791.

54   Pat Alderman, *The Overmountain Men* (Johnson City, TN: The Overmountain Press, 1970), 123.

55   Grant #1220. 329, 29 July 1793, 200 acres on Sinking Creek Fork of Lick Creek adj Drew Morris and Shadrach Morris.

56   North Carolina Grant #54, Washington Co, 1783—Alexander Campbell, 100 acres

the waters of Little Limestone Creek."[57] The fourth grant, in 1783, calls for 200 acres "on the waters of Big Limestone."[58]

In August 1788, when David was two years old, John Crockett embarked with Brigadier General Joseph Martin and about eight hundred men on an ill-fated campaign against Chief Dragging Canoe, the scourge of frontier settlements and chief of the Chickamauga branch of the Cherokee tribe.

Joseph Martin had taken a Cherokee wife, Betsey Ward, the daughter of Chief Nancy Ward and her second husband, English trader Bryant Ward. Virginia governor Patrick Henry had appointed Martin as the Indian Agent to the Cherokees. This position had brought him even closer to the Wards, as well as the revered chief Oconostota, the "Little Carpenter." Because of these ties, some agitating settlers perceived Martin as favoring Indian interests at the expense of their own.

There had been a rift between Martin and John Sevier. In addition, Martin had allied himself with the state of North Carolina during the contentious struggle over the failed State of Franklin. The campaign against Chief Dragging Canoe and the Chickamaugas did not succeed, primarily because the men would not accept Martin's leadership. After some unexpected resistance by the Chickamaugas, the men refused to take orders from Martin or to take the offensive. Martin had no choice but to return home. Other men connected with the Limestone neighborhood who served under Martin in this expedition included Captain Thomas Gillespie (Cert. No. 629) and James Stinson, Sr. and Jr. (Certs. No. 608 & 617).

John Crockett was a Franklinite and his certificate number (given to troops who took part in this campaign) was No. 1026. His certificate

---

"on both sides of great Limestone Creek."

57   North Carolina Grant #69, Washington Co, 1783—Alexander Campbell, 207 acres "on the waters of Little Limestone Creek."

58   North Carolina Grant #585, Washington Co, 1783—Alexander Campbell, 200 acres "on the waters of Big Limestone."

reflects the rank of *Serjt* (or sergeant).[59] There were only twelve such sergeant designations, which would indicate that John Crockett was considered a leader within the militia group, given the low number of men who carried such a designation.

A total of only thirty-three officers were listed from a corps of some eight hundred men. Other officers under which John served included Captain James Moore, Lieutenant Cornelius Newman, and Ensign James Robinson (the only officer of this rank). These unit members had consecutive certificate numbers: from Captain Moore at number 1023 to Sergeant John Crockett at number 1026.

There are no records to indicate John Crockett's loyalties, except for his Franklin association. Greene County was a bastion of Franklin support, the capital being at Greeneville. We know of no Crockett ties to John Sevier, save the erroneous statements concerning the relation of their wives. General Joseph Martin was the ranking officer at Fort Lee, very near to John Crockett's home.

Even though Indians massacred his parents, we have no indication that John Crockett bore particular animosity to Indians as a group or would have been labeled as an "Indian hater," a designation that would apply to other members of the campaign.

---

59   NC Revolutionary Army Accounts Vol. VI and Book No. 39 Treasurer's & Comptroller's Papers, Military Papers, Indian Wars 1788-1798. North Carolina state Archives, Raleigh. Cert No. 1026—"John Crockett, Serjt, 6 17 6."

CHAPTER 4:

The Early Frontier Landscape and Life in East Tennessee

What is known today as East Tennessee was the domain of the Cherokee prior to European arrival, though much of the land to the north and west (between the Tennessee and the Ohio Rivers), was used as hunting grounds by various indigenous tribes. The Cherokee, Shawnee, Creek, and Chickasaw all hunted there. Native tribes were dispersed across the region and had first encounters or conflicts with Europeans at all four directions of the compass. The Iroquois and the Shawnee occupied the north; the Chickasaw met and held off the Spanish and the French from the Mississippi; the Creek, Choctaw, and Seminole blocked the area from the southern gulf. The Cherokee guarded the route from the Carolinas and the Shenandoah Valley. Conflict among the tribes was usual. In the early 1700s, the Cherokee and the Chickasaw were allies against the individual incursions of the Shawnee from the north and the Creeks from the south.

Tennessee historian J. G. M. Ramsey preserved for posterity many of the names used by the Cherokee to designate landmarks in the territory now known as East Tennessee. They were:

… names remarkable for their euphony and beauty …
Alaghnee, Unaca, Chilhowee, and *Chattanooga.* Later
European place-names like Dumplin, Sandy Mush, Little
Dismal, Bull Run, Calf Killer, … etc., would grate harshly
upon the ears of the Cherokee.[60]

Naming of rivers in early Tennessee was a cosmopolitan affair,
though, with French names as well as English and Indian names seen
on early maps. The French called the Tennessee River *Reviere des
Chraquis.* The Cherokee had named the Little Tennessee River the
Tannassee. Other river names included the Holston (*Hogeehogee*) and
the French Broad (*Taquastah*). The Tennessee River from its mouth
at the Ohio River to the mouth of the Little Tennessee River was
called the *Kallamuchee;* but from the Little Tennessee to the mouth
of the French Broad, the Tennessee River was called the *Cootela.* The
Nolichucky was the *Nonachunkeh*; the Pigeon River—*Agiqua.* Little
River was known as the *Canot,* and the Tellico was called the *Ptsaliko*
or *Saliko* (named for the daughter of Chief Unaka). The Hiwasee was
pronounced *Euphasee.* The Watauga River's aboriginal name was
Conesauga.[61]

Later, white settlers would label the landscape with simple work-
aday names like First Creek or Second Creek, Knob Creek, Sinking
Creek, Flat Creek, or Bent Creek. Mountains would receive short
and descriptive names like Stone Mountain, Pine Mountain, Short
Mountain, or Green Mountain. Simple names like Little River or
Broad River might be added to historian Ramsey's view that settlers
cared little for euphony, or "words pleasing to the ear," in naming the
mountains and rivers around them.

Along rivers and wetlands, one found great stands of *Arundinaria
gigantea* or "river cane," generally around low-lying creeks or river
bottoms. A species of bamboo, river cane has a pithy, hollow stem

60   J. G. M. Ramsey, *Annals of Tennessee* (Charleston, SC: Walker & Jones, 1853), 86.

61   Ramsey, *Annals of Tennessee,* 87.

and grows in tight "canebrake" outcroppings along water features. It was used widely by Indian tribes to make shelters, baskets, rope, and weapons like spears or blow guns. Cane was a food staple for the woodland bison that roamed the area. As an evergreen crop, cane was important as a winter food source for White settlers' horses and cattle. Today, cane can still be seen in a few small patches along river and stream banks in East Tennessee, but the large canebrakes have all but vanished.

David Crockett came to be known by many monikers during his forty-nine years of life and after. One of the more accurate, though not initially well-received by Crockett himself, was "The Gentleman from the Cane." During the 1821 Tennessee legislative session, "a snobbish gentleman from the eastern part of the state, a Mr. James C. Mitchell, publicly referred to Crockett as 'the gentleman from the cane.' The legislative chamber erupted in laughter, the kind of smug laughter that insiders use against an outsider. Being from 'the cane,' the cane brakes, was the equivalent of being a hillbilly; it was an insult based on class distinctions, and Crockett was stung."[62]

Though Crockett initially intended to thrash Mitchell for his insolence, he found a better alternative: soon after, Crockett appeared on the legislative floor wearing a frilly shirt ruffle of the kind worn by his pretentious antagonist. "It was a brilliant stroke of comeuppance, for suddenly the humor of the situation dawned upon all the members and without a word being uttered, they all burst out laughing. Crockett had found a way of ridiculing his adversary without whaling the daylights out of him, and his fellow legislators let him know they appreciated his ingenuity."[63] Mitchell withdrew from the chamber in humiliation, and Crockett thereafter wore the title of "The Gentleman from the Cane" with a degree of pride, often reminding people of his nickname if they didn't bring it up first.

---

62   Jesse A. Jones, "Say it ain't true, Davy! The Real David Crockett vs. The Backwoodsman in Us All," *Appalachian Journal* Vol. 15, no. 1 (Fall 1987):45–51.

63   Jones, "Say it ain't true, Davy!," 45–51.

Wildlife like buffalo, deer, and elk (as well as domesticated farm animals) seek out salt. Buffalo and deer were often the first to identify salt springs, which Indians and settlers knew as "salt licks" or "salt-sulfur licks," and visited themselves to collect the valuable mineral. Buffalo trails naturally led to and from these salt licks. The town of Nashville, Tennessee, was founded at what was originally known as French Lick.[64]

Wildlife and Forested Landscape

Prior to the arrival of Europeans, Native American populations made great use of the plentiful nuts from hickory, walnut, or chestnut trees. They would mash and boil the nuts to render off an oil used in cooking. Wild strawberries, blueberries, and blackberries were also abundant, and the tribes were said to have cultivated plum, persimmon, and peach trees.

Turkey and grouse were common. Flocks of wild pigeons (*Ectopistes migratorius,* later known as passenger pigeons) were so large, they were said to darken the sun. Large deer populations provided ample food supply to native peoples (as well as for timber wolves and mountain lions). Smaller animals like beaver, mink, river otters, muskrats, squirrels, and rabbits were abundant, and provided many a meal for birds of prey like eagles, owls, and hawks, as well as for wildcats, red wolves, and foxes. Stream-fed beaver ponds created natural habitat for waterfowl that included swans, geese, and ducks, as well as fish.

Other habitat for fish included cold-water mountain streams that were teeming with native Appalachian brook trout, called *specs* by the mountaineers for the multicolored small spots on their sides. These small but feisty native fish averaged about eight inches in length and have always been considered a rare culinary delight. This species is

---

64   Samuel Cole Williams, *Dawn of Tennessee Valley and Tennessee History* (Johnson City, TN: Wautaga Press, 1937), 51.

actually not trout at all, but a variety of arctic char. They were very common into the early 1900s and easy prey even for a boy with a crude cane pole. The introduction and proliferation of brown and rainbow trout from Europe (about 1920) greatly diminished their numbers. They're found in higher elevation streams today.

Other fish populated rivers like the French Broad, Holston, Little Tennessee, and the Tennessee River. One could find populations of river sturgeon, a survivor of the ice age, that could approach a hundred pounds and could live to be over a hundred years old. Sturgeon proved to be sensitive to human pollution: man-made dams disrupted their spawning migrations and few sturgeon remain today.

The early frontier saw a variety of large mammals on its landscape. Eastern woodland bison foraged in the valleys east of the Mississippi River in numbers that may have approached four million. Daniel Boone tells of seeing rare traces of the buffalo in the 1760s on trails in the Watauga River area in upper East Tennessee. Place names like "Buffalo Wallow," near the Crockett home in Finley Gap, are common in Tennessee, and hark back to the days when the land was thick with the wooly bovines, which vanished so quickly with the advent of market hunting. Bison were largely extirpated from Tennessee by 1823.[65]

This ecosystem that took millennia to develop was changed dramatically by the pressure brought about by European migration into the territory. The numbers of large game animals fell rapidly with the arrival of White hunters, both subsistence and market hunters. Among the first species to vanish were the buffalo and the elk. The deer herd was steadily reduced in number, which depleted not only an important settler and Native food source, but also had adverse effects on larger carnivore predators like the mountain lion and wolf. The loss of primary food sources, along with bounties paid on wolf pelts, and organized hunts like the one David mentions on page 62 of his *Narrative* drove the red wolves and timber wolves out completely by

---

65   "Bison Bellows: Bison East of The Mississippi," National Park Service, https://www.nps.gov/articles/bison-bellows-9-16-16.htm.

an early date. While a number of wildlife species have vanished from the region entirely, elk began to be reintroduced to Tennessee in the late 1900s.

The varied patterns and density of Tennessee woodlands provided habitat to a variety of wildlife, with the landscape favoring old-growth trees with a high canopy and very little brush or understory. Fire is a natural and perennial agent on the landscape, where blazes sparked by lightning burn through and clear out brush under the canopy, leaving the large thick-barked trees undamaged. Tornadoes and blow-downs disrupted the forest cover, opening up the canopy and allowing light to reach the forest floor. This natural environmental activity led to a patchwork environment of forests that were dense in places and had open areas and even meadows in others.

Manifest Destiny

The great flood of European settlers into the American west would become associated with the cultural belief of "manifest destiny." There was a price to be paid for this destiny, however. Motivated primarily by the material self-interest of settlers arriving from the Eastern Seaboard, the land saw the almost complete destruction of Native cultures and populations. The very character of the land was changed and continues to be to this day.

Roads and Bison Traces

Settlers arriving in early Tennessee often traveled the road that started in central Pennsylvania and traveled down the Shenandoah Valley of Virginia, continuing through the valleys of East Tennessee to the area around present-day Chattanooga. The path was an ancient one. It began thousands of years ago and followed the lines of bison migrations. Often referred to as "buffalo," the North American bison (scientific name *Bison bison*, from the Latin word for "wild ox") could weigh in at two thousand pounds for a male and about one thousand pounds for a female. Their weight and sharp hooves packed the soil along their migratory routes, leaving a trail or "trace" that could be twenty feet wide and compacted several feet deep in places.

Bison proved to be excellent pathfinders, establishing paths of least resistance over mountains and across plains and streams. Native Americans then used these paths as trading and war trails, one of which became known as the "Great Indian Warpath" (also known as the "Great Indian War and Trading Path," or the "Seneca Trail"). This trail is still visible in places as it winds along the ridges, creeks, and rivers along the western foothills of the Appalachians. Interstate Highway 81 travels right through the youthful Crockett's old paths along the Shenandoah, and US Highway 11E follows the course of Indian, bison, and game trails, as do many highways across the nation today.

Dutch (German) and Ulster-Scots families like the Crocketts would follow the road to the frontier's extreme edge before stopping, carrying with them indispensable equipment such as rifle, powder, and shot, and implements like a hoe and axe. Travel by road into the frontier was typically by foot, astride horse or mule, or leading horse- or mule-drawn wagon. In the early days of settlement, roads were needed to facilitate commerce between settlements. As communities were established, county legislative bodies oversaw the creation and maintenance of these roads, appointing "overseers" and employing neighborhood men to perform the work of maintaining the roads.

American Frontier Life

The "Great Wagon Road" from Washington to Knoxville during this period from 1770 to 1810 was *the* road to the south and west, following along the west side of the Appalachian Mountains (a course followed by Interstate 81 today). People who lived along the road and those who regularly traveled the road came to know each other, as the speed of travel allowed passersby time to converse as they gathered at taverns and ferry crossings along the way. The great migration of the Ulster-Scots followed this road from central and western Pennsylvania to eastern Tennessee in huge numbers. Even those traveling to Kentucky mostly came first into East Tennessee and then up through the Cumberland Gap.

For the pioneers, the most important trees were the chestnut and the old-growth yellow pines. The chestnut wood was workable and provided a strong, flexible, and weather-resistant resource for making tools, wagons, barrels, and tool handles. The nuts from the chestnut fed untold numbers of species, which in turn fed the pioneers. The old-growth pines were dense and rich in rosin, providing weather-resistant heartwood that was soft enough to be easily worked into roof shingles, floorboards, and furniture.

Over two hundred years, much of Tennessee's original forest was harvested for human use. The old-growth pine trees take centuries to grow, and once the virgin forests were cut, these trees were no more. Plantings of fast-growing, lower-quality trees have taken the place of the far superior old-growth heartwood trees, exchanging quality for greatly increased quantity. While reforestation efforts have occurred, Tennessee today has few large stands of old-growth trees (outside of the Great Smoky Mountains).[66]

A pioneer family's first shelter on a new homestead was very basic in form, consisting typically of a square or rectangular hut made of poles and bark, with one open side where a fire would be built for cooking and warmth in cold weather. A pioneer cabin provided protection from mosquitoes, ticks, snakes, and other animals in warm weather. Food was also basic, consisting of salted pork, beef, and game, supplemented by potatoes and corn bread. When long journeys were undertaken, parched corn carried well and was a staple.

These foods were augmented by the natural bounty that surrounded them. Like the native population, settlers hunted the abundant game,

---

66   Jim Brown, Forester, U. S. Forest Service. *The Timber and Vegetation of the Appalachian Region of East Tennessee and Western North Carolina in the Pioneer Period—1700 to 1850.*

and gathered nuts, berries, herbs, roots, and plants that grew wild in season. Daily activities started well before sunrise, with rekindling of fires and the cooking of the most important meal of the day: breakfast. Daily activities included clearing land; planting, tending, and reaping crops; caring for animals; constructing and maintaining fences; cutting and gathering firewood; building and maintaining shelters for the family and livestock; storing food, hay, and grain; and eventually slaughtering livestock and preserving foods of all kinds.

Women performed many of these tasks, all while also caring for the children and managing the household. Clothes had to be made from hand. Women handled the food processing and preparation, tended fires, carried water, and made soap and candles.

The women watched out for the community's small children, who were subjected to dangers from diseases to accidents. With few if any doctors on the frontier, parents were left mostly to treat sicknesses and injury. Neighbors often pooled their resources and those who were more knowledgeable in healing would be called upon to help with injuries or illnesses of others.

In addition to the normal daily challenges, early pioneers faced routine problems of nature and the weather. Floods often washed out months of hard work on crops and buildings, while drought and predators were a constant threat to crops and livestock. There were constant dangers associated with Native Americans, who correctly saw the settlers as trespassers and treaty violators.

For the early settlers, this landscape presented a bounty of opportunities and resources. Those immense resources, however, could demand a weighty price. The struggles of the Crockett family, and so many others like them, bear witness to the pitfalls and the wonders of this great and terrible time in man's struggle to balance opportunity for a better life with the unknown dangers of an all-too-often unforgiving frontier.

Life on the frontier was hard and dangerous. Time moved at a slower pace. Tools had to be fashioned by hand. Even the rudest forms of automation were unknown on the frontier. To clothe themselves, settlers had to start with the most basic of materials like leather, wool, flax, and linen. These products themselves had to be processed from animals and crops. Clothing and footwear were crafted using thread and binding materials that *also* had to be made by hand. To work their crops, farm implements had to either be imported or built on the scene, using available wood, iron, leather, and rope. Crops required harvesting, processing, and storage to be on hand to feed the family through the long, cold winters.

Another daily duty on the frontier was the tending of livestock, which involved building fences, and doctoring, protecting, pasturing, feeding, shearing, and milking them—and eventually slaughtering them and preserving the meat. Horses, mules, and oxen were common draft animals and required daily care. Livestock tack and implements like harnesses, yokes, saddles, sleds, and wagons had to be constructed or procured.

These early residents of the western frontier quickly cultivated a taste for two things that were readily available: pork and corn whiskey. Early Scots historically had shunned pork, but this changed when they came to the frontier, and pork became their meat of preference. Virtually every homestead had pigs, most of which roamed freely. As a consequence, large numbers of domesticated pigs escaped and went feral. Hunting wild hogs for sport and table became (and still is) quite popular, so much so that the small-bore muzzle-loading rifle became known as a "Tennessee Hog Rifle."

It did not take the settlers long to learn how to turn their new corn crop into corn whiskey. The process was not complicated, nor was whiskey expensive to produce. Distilleries or "stills" were abundant, and corn liquor was an expected refreshment at most social gatherings. Many social norms were modified by a rough life on the frontier, and overdrinking (or "being in your cups") was a common problem. The absence of social pressures and formal regulations on alcohol and its consumption left the door open to abuse and gave rise to organized temperance movements in the 1820s and 1830s.

Summary of Frontier Life

From 1840 is an account of a man who came to stay at the Montvale Springs Hotel at the base of the Chilhowee Mountains near Maryville in Blount County, TN (approximately forty miles southwest of the Finley neighborhood in Bays Mountain of Jefferson County). He gave his impression of Tennessee settlers:

> The Tennessean is, in person, generally tall and godly featured, not inclined to corpulence, but muscular and active, the men can scarcely be termed over industrious. The leading crop was Indian corn, which they commence planting the latter end of March: it has to be kept very clean, and requires four and five ploughings, which occupies them until the end of June. The Wheat, Oat, and Hay Harvest then commences, and is usually completed by the middle of July; after that, to ride about, gossip, fish, hunt, and shoot, engrosses their leading attention (fodder and corn pulling, and wheat sowing excepted) until March again. The women are more industrious, their attention, and that of their household, is occupied the year round (exclusive of the time required for domestic duties) in carding, spinning, dying, and weaving, woolen cotton and flax cloth, which, after clothing themselves, children, domestics, and out servants with, they sell or barter to the storekeeper, thus realizing the description in Prov. v. 13 "She maketh fine linen and selleth it, and delivereth her girdles to the merchant."[67]

The settlers had traveled from a world dominated by villages and communities on the eastern coast of America (or in the Scots, Irish, or British lands from which they migrated) to a frontier where neighbors

---

67   J. Gray Smith, *Review of East Tennessee or A Brief Historical, Statistical, and Descriptive Review of East Tennessee, United States of America: Developing Its Immense Agricultural, Mining, and Manufacturing Advantages, with Remarks to Emigrants, 1842.* Reprinted by The Reprint Company, Spartanburg, SC, 1974.

and settlements were isolated and miles apart. This social structure lent itself to the pioneer who prioritized his family and his close community and took initiative in work and personal standards of conduct.

Frontier life was hard and gritty, frequently testing the limits of human endurance, strength, and energy. For the John Crockett family, and may others like them, it was a fight from dawn to dusk just to scratch out a meager existence of basic food and shelter. But for most, the resources and abundance available offered the chance for a life better than the one they had left behind in Pennsylvania or Virginia. The risks were great, but so were the potential rewards. Those who survived were stronger and tougher for the experience.

The body of knowledge these people brought with them had been accumulated over a very long time. Their closeness to, and understanding of, nature was so much more personal than ours today because they lived so much closer to it. The Native population lived even more intimately with the natural elements than their White neighbors did.

Today in East Tennessee, no longer a frontier, one can take the Chucky Pike up the south slope to the top of Bays Mountain and down through Finley Gap to the East Dumplin Valley Road that passes the site of the Finley home, and later nearby, David's first home. As you view the land spreading out into the Dumplin Creek Valley along the north face of Bays Mountain, you can still see much of it as the early pioneers saw it. Looking out across that valley as you turn left onto the East Dumplin Valley Road, you'll find early morning mist settling onto fields at the base of the mountain. If you look hard enough, you can find the grave of David's father-in-law, Billy Finley.

The land looks much the same today as it did when the Indians traveled the ancient Great Indian War Trail that crossed Bays Mountain. It looks much as it did in 1818 when they laid Billy in his final resting place. One can hear the sounds and feel the fog and mist rolling off the ridges of Bays Mountain, with the smell of moist sweet grass on a spring or fall morning. The senses convey a feeling of quietness and timelessness of the Tennessee landscape.

CHAPTER 5:

The Scot and Irish Roots of the Crocketts

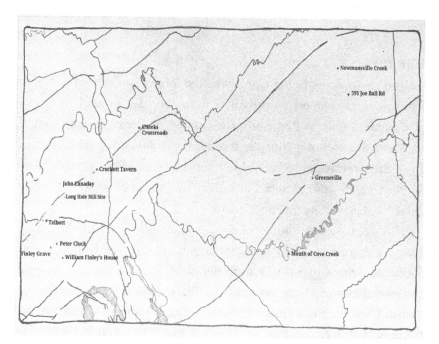

Many eighteenth-century immigrants who came from England, Scotland, and Ireland made their way from America's Eastern Seaboard, across the Appalachians and into the present-day states of Kentucky and Tennessee. Families like the Scots-Irish Crocketts brought their culture with them.

The original name of "Crockett" may have derived from the ancient Norse word *krok-r*, meaning "crook," "hook," or "bend," and is probably the root word of the old English word *crock*. In Gothic architecture, a *crocket* is a small ornament projecting from the sloping angles of pinnacles or spires, and typically depict stylized foliage. It was typical for the spellings of family names to change over time, and the name of Crockett was no exception. Common variations of "Crockett" can be found as *Crocket, Croket, Crocit* or *Crokit*. Other Scottish spellings like *Crockete, Crokat,* or *Crockitt* were also common. While David professed his opinion that the middle *c* and the extra *t* were unnecessary (preferring a spelling of *Croket*), he nevertheless was consistent in spelling his family name as *Crockett* when signing in his own hand. [68]

The Picts

According to *Scots in the Carolinas*, the largest number of Crockett families in the Americas migrated from the area around the town of Coupar Angus in Perthshire (or County of Perth) in east central Scotland. Located north of the mouth of the River Tay (the Firth of Tay), this area is one of the oldest settled areas of the British Isles. Scottish kings were crowned at nearby Moot Hill close to the Scone Palace as far back as the ninth century A.D.[69]

This area was the home of the Southern Picts, an ethnic group whose culture flourished from sometime prior to the Roman occupation of Britain in 50 A.D. until the ninth or tenth century. Known by the Romans as "Caledonians," the Picts were the only tribe in the British Isles that the Romans failed to subdue. Hadrian's Wall and the Antonin Wall were built to hold out the Picts. The Antonin Wall was overrun almost as soon as it was built. The seventy-three-mile-long

---

68   John Gadsby Chapman, Journal of Crockett portrait, 1834.

69   David Dobson, *Directory of Scots in the Carolinas* (Baltimore: Clearfield Co., 2009), 52.

Hadrian's Wall, built near the border between Scotland and England, was finished about 122 A.D. Although breached at times, Hadrian's Wall proved an effective defense and was garrisoned, fortified, and maintained over many years.

The characteristics of these early Picts are interesting, considering what is known about David Crockett. The Picts had a great love for hounds and have been described as wily and stealthy with the ability to quickly disappear into the highlands without a trace. Pictish men were described as powerfully built, with short legs, barrel chests, dark skin, dark hair and eyes. They were feared as extraordinary fighters with great physical strength and stamina.

English and Scotch Incursions into Ireland

Large numbers of Scots, including the Crockett clan, came from Galloway, Lanark, Renfrew, and Ayr along the Scottish borders, with others coming from further north in the Scottish Lowlands. Seeking opportunity, they seized upon the plantation of Ulster as the best available option in their desperate situation. The official plantation comprised an estimated half a million acres of land in the Irish counties of Armagh, Cavan, Fermanagh, Tyrone, Tyrconnell, and Londonderry. Lands in Antrim, Monaghan, and Down were also privately colonized with the support and encouragement of the English monarchy.

The Ulster-Scots were originally Scots and North Britons who were encouraged by the English government to migrate on a large scale to the area of Ulster in Northern Ireland during the 1600s for the purpose of helping to hold lands confiscated from malcontent Irish lords by the English monarchy. Although predominantly Celtic Scots (ethnically more like the English), the Ulster-Scots also included a number of Gaelic Highland Scots, who shared an early ancestry with the natives of Ireland.

In recent years, genetic links between the Scots and inhabitants of Ireland have been noted. The number of families who lived in both Ireland and Scotland at different times and generations may be larger than the prevailing common knowledge would have noted a few decades ago. The Scots and Irish are an interesting mix of Celtic, Gaelic, and Scandinavian heritage. The lowland Scots were a mixture of Celts, Romans, Scandinavians, Germans, English, Irish, and Scots. The area of southern Scotland and northern England was an age-old battleground known as the Border region where lawlessness became a way of life for many who lived there. The residents of this contested landscape raided back and forth across the border from before the time of the Romans in the first century A.D. This lawlessness and fighting had, if anything, escalated by the seventeenth century, creating an environment of strife and disorder, which effectively undermined any kind of sustained economic opportunity.

The predominantly Presbyterian Scots who were transplanted into the confiscated areas of Northern Ireland known as Ulster brought with them a bitter dislike for the Pope and the Roman Catholic Church. Not surprisingly, an intense animosity between the transplanted Protestant Scots and the dispossessed Irish Catholics resulted. Continued attempts by the Irish to isolate and eradicate the Scots made them, out of necessity, more rigid, rugged, self-reliant, and self-sufficient.

Generations of Scots were successful in developing the war-torn and poverty-stricken lands around Ulster/Londonderry into a thriving industrial region. Their English landlords began to employ a policy referred to as *rack-renting*: doubling or tripling rents in now well-developed areas.

From the time between the initial plantation in 1610 until about 1660, Northern Ireland was a hellish place to live. Wars of rebellion and the confiscation of land from the native Irish were granted to a variety of English insiders and investors, resulting in the displacement of native Irish by Scotch and English settlers. This social conflict resulted in the creation of a number of murderous warring factions, fueled by plots and intrigues from powerful insiders who were often part of the English government, all fighting each other for control of the turbulent Irish landscape. The English and native Irish landholders postured to gain advantage, resulting in attacks and reprisals that took untold numbers of lives in a climate of fear, instability, and destruction. During this time, mostly native Catholic land ownership fell from around 60 percent to a low of about 9 percent in 1660 at the end of the English Commonwealth period under Cromwell.

Sir William Petty, a statistician of the period, wrote that during this period, out of a population in Ireland of 1,448,000, a staggering 616,000 (42 percent) had perished by sword, famine, or plague. Petty says that before 1641, about two-thirds of the land was in possession of the Catholics. By 1660, two-thirds were in the possession of insurgent Protestants. "The tribal organization of Ireland that had shown vitality for more than a millennium was destroyed *root and branch*, never to return."[70]

Impetus to Migration

These events were the genesis of what we today recognize as the great Scots-Irish migration from Northern Ireland to America. Being oppressed socially, religiously, politically, but primarily economically, they moved on again to America. Those who migrated out of this region came mostly from the areas around Ulster. They crossed the Atlantic, with many arriving in Pennsylvania, eventually making their way down the Shenandoah Valley of Virginia into the Carolinas and Tennessee. This migration began during the 1680s and 1690s, as tens of thousands of Lowland and Border Scots fled catastrophic famine in those areas. Migrations continued as over a quarter million people moved to America during the years 1718 to 1775. By the time they arrived on the northeastern coast of America, much of the best farming lands had already been claimed. Thus, the Scots-Irish immigrants began to settle in south central Pennsylvania on the western edge of the frontier.

The old world that these pioneers left behind had a specific social

---

70   Henry Jones Ford, *The Scotch-Irish in America* (Princeton: Princeton University Press, 1915), 116.

order upon which the stability of society depended. They were basically divided into two groups: the well-to-do without title and the lower classes. When the Ulster-Scots arrived in America, social hierarchies were in place, which was the exact circumstance they were fleeing in the old world. The people inhabiting America up until the Revolutionary War were still tied to the old order and customs. This situation was a prime motivator among the Ulster-Scots to find a place of their own where they could achieve a reasonable measure of economic freedom and opportunity.

The word *clannish* was used to describe these Scots for good reason. They were more than a little intolerant by nature and they did not like the strange language to which the German immigrants clung, nor the strict doctrines of Quakers already settled in Pennsylvania. It is said of the Ulster-Scots that they were not prejudiced against any particular group—but held all those different from themselves in contempt equally. The Ulster-Scots were primarily Presbyterian and many practiced religious bigotry with a particular zeal common during this period.

The story of Anglican minister Charles Woodmason illustrated the bigotry practiced by the Presbyterian Ulster-Scots. Woodmason was traveling the backcountry, preaching to communities along the way. As he tried to give an Anglican sermon, the Presbyterians rioted outside the church during his service. They started a pack of dogs to fighting, gave his congregation two barrels of whiskey before a communion service, stole his church key, and turned his horse loose. Running an Anglican minister out of town certainly inspired creativity among the often-taciturn Presbyterians.

Patterns of Western Migration

As the Ulster-Scots continued to search for available lands on which to farm, they began migrating south and west along the shadow of the Blue Ridge Mountains. They moved along the Shenandoah Valley and into the mountains and piedmont of North Carolina, the upcountry of

South Carolina, and on into northern Georgia. Their westerly course of migration took them into the mountains and hills of what would become Tennessee. The prolific annual rainfall in this mountainous country fed numerous streams and springs. The easy availability of water allowed the settlers to lay off independent family farms, which spread quickly across the region. These circumstances encouraged their propensity for a stubborn autonomy.

The Ulster-Scots left their mark on the history and in memorials on the lands they staked out as their own. For example, in the Mount Horeb Presbyterian Cemetery in Jefferson County, Tennessee (about a mile from the childhood home of David's wife, Polly Finley Crockett), there is a marker commemorating the Scots-Irish Rankin family, one of the earliest pioneer families in eastern Tennessee. The Rankins, who had settled in the Dumplin Valley of Jefferson County, at the foot of Bays Mountain, left a marker that spoke of the Ulster-Scots exodus. It reads in part:

> This Tablet is to Commemorate the Memory of Richard Rankin 1756-1827; Samuel Rankin 1758-1828; Thomas Rankin 1762-1821; John Bradshaw 1743-1818.

The marker goes on to record:

> Alexander Rankin born in Scotland had three sons, two were martyred to their religion. Of these one was killed on the highway, the other suffocated in a smokehouse where he had taken refuge to escape from his pursuers. The third brother, William, together with his father and family escaped to Derry County, Ireland. In 1688 William and his father were participants in the siege of Londonderry which took place in 1689.

Of the Rankin family's second generation:

> William Rankin had three sons, Adam born in Scotland,
> 1689, John and Hugh born in Ireland. Adam and Hugh came
> to America in 1721 landing in Philadelphia, Pa., and settled
> in Chester County [Pennsylvania].

Of their third generation:

> John Rankin married Jane McElwee, in Ireland, came to
> America in 1727. He had two sons Thomas and Richard
> and eight daughters.

The primary pattern of western migration of the Ulster-Scots from Pennsylvania followed along the Shenandoah Valley of Virginia and continued south and west into Tennessee (or over into North Carolina, then to Tennessee, as the Crocketts and many others did). These settlers were often accompanied by a smaller contingent of Germanic settlers, each group leap-frogging their way across the frontier.

Many of these Scots migrated as whole congregations or family groups, along with their Presbyterian ministers. The extended family units were extremely tight-knit, a very important factor considering the scale of this group's migrations. It was quite common for whole communities of these Scots-Irish pioneers to migrate along the same routes, stopping at the same places along the way.

Jumping from one conflict to another, many of these Ulster-Scots were no strangers to hostile environments. They began moving across the mountain barrier and into the lands of long-established Native American tribes. As their numbers grew, so did the tensions with the native populations. Three primary forts emerged as the newly arrived settlers moved across the frontier: Fort Caswell (Watauga) on the Watauga River, Eaton's Station at Carter's Valley, and Fort Lee on the Nolichucky River near Limestone.

Character of the Scottish Immigrants in America

The early Scottish immigrants to America had deep experience being isolated in hostile environments. The hard experiences they had endured while fighting with the English and with each other in their homeland (and with the native Irish in Ulster) had tempered their spirits and stiffened their resolve, making them no stranger to the precarious conditions of the new frontier in front of them. In America, when not fighting among themselves, the Scots-Irish immigrants turned their attention to the Native Americans, often with the same kind of murderous zeal they had employed in the old homeland.

Many of these immigrants were poor but bestowed with a fierce and stubborn pride that chafed at any hint of disrespect. While they were tough, they were also adventurous and versatile, and among themselves, demonstrated sharp wit and a keen sense of humor, often joking, teasing, and arguing. Among their own kind, they were gregarious and fun-loving and often preferred self-sufficient isolationism.

These Ulster-Scots were well-known as a distinct frontier group, pragmatic by nature and necessity. Many other newly arrived European settlers learned to steer clear of them. Most of the Ulster-Scots migrants did not allow themselves the luxury of pondering questions of ethics and morality, and they were not generally prone to caution and deliberation. They understood that life was hard, as it had always been for them and their forebears, and especially for the women and children. Life expectancy was significantly skewed in favor of adult males.

The Scots-Irish of early America had a defiant spirit, in spite of years of living in poverty and servitude. Their desire for freedom and liberty were engendered by their previous generations who had not enjoyed those qualities of life. Simply existing in America did not guarantee their being free from poverty, debt, or servitude. Yet the Scots-Irish of early America knew they had a chance in this new land to earn their freedom and prosperity—if they used their wits, good sense, skills of hard work, and some luck. Opportunities abounded for those willing to take risks, even if not "calculated risks" and instead jump-off-and-see-where-you-land kind of risks. They valued traits like intuition and instinct, recklessness, toughness, humor, endurance, perseverance, loyalty, and tenacity. Spontaniety abounded and they seldom developed detailed plans. Many were devoted to their religion, but few incorporated religion into their daily lives (as the Quakers did).

Within this group of settlers was a kind of renegade hierarchy or social order, a system in which a few families rose to prominence. These families often obtained their wealth and position by living on the outskirts of the law. Such is the case with the families of the Grahams and the Bells, who were forcibly moved from the northwest of England to Ireland. After immigrating to America, they maintained their status of wealth and power both in Ireland and America. The families of Andrew Jackson, James Polk, Sam Houston, and many others who achieved prominence in early America came from such a background. These few used advantages of wealth and power on these frontier lands, which they leveraged to greater status in early America.

David Crockett was not born with these advantages. In fact, it took his second marriage to attain the capital and status necessary to make possible his career as a politician on the national level.

CHAPTER 6:

Military Service of John Crockett, the Overmountain Scots, and the Battle of Kings Mountain

The fighting spirit of early Scots-Irish immigrants, a group which included David's father, John Crockett, made these men valued contributors in the fight for American independence. As John Crockett and his brothers William, Robert, and Alexander reached maturity during the American Revolution, the turmoil of the period and their experience at arms would propel them forward into a life on the frontier. In their path lay Native Americans: some initially welcoming, some understandably hostile to waves of European settlers rolling into their ancestral lands, and some allying themselves with the British in efforts to hold back the surge of migrants moving west into territory where the Indians had lived for more than ten thousand years.

Both Indians and Whites suffered in these violent clashes. In 1777, when John Crockett was away as a militia ranger, his mother and father (David's grandparents) were killed by marauding Cherokee and Creek Indians allied with the British at the site of what is now Rogersville, Tennessee. The tribes were attempting to stop the White advance and to drive encroaching settlers from land long occupied by the Cherokees and Creeks. Of David's memories of his father's Revolutionary War service, he noted:

> I have an imperfect recollection of the part which I have understood my father took in the revolutionary war. … I have learned that he was a soldier in the revolutionary war, and took part in that bloody struggle. He fought, according to my information, in the battle at Kings Mountain against the British and Tories, and in some other engagements of which my remembrance is too imperfect to enable me to speak. [N, 2]

Military and Civil Service of Crockett Forebears

Crockett's father, John, and a number of his uncles served in a military capacity or in other positions of service to their communities. In a 1921 article in the *Daughters of the American Revolution Magazine*, author Louise Reynolds stated that John Crockett was a frontier ranger during the war, and she also noted that he participated in the battle at Kings Mountain (adding again that John Crockett may have been in Pennsylvania as a ranger at the time his parents were killed in the attack at Rogersville).[71] In his book *The Overmountain Men*, author Pat Alderman stated that brothers John, William, Robert, and Alexander Crockett served under Col. Isaac Shelby in the pivotal Battle of Kings Mountain.[72]

In 1833, John's next older brother Robert Crockett filed for a Revolutionary War pension at the age of 78. In his pension deposition

---

71   Reynolds, "The Pioneer Crockett Family, " 188.

72   Alderman, *The Overmountain Men*, 120.

dated June 7, 1832, Robert gave a detailed account of his Revolutionary War activities: [73]

- June 1776—Served 1 month along the North Carolina frontier as a substitute for Jacob Willes under Capt. James Johnson and Col. Wm. Grimes
- 1776—Served under Capt. Isaac Blitcher 3 months building a fort on the frontier of Sullivan County, Tennessee
- 1777—A draftsman for Capt. Wm. Asher for 3 months
- 1778—Served 7 weeks in the Campaign to the Chickamauga Country under Col. Evan Shelby and Capt. Bledsoe
- 1780—Drafted for 2 months during which time he fought in the Battle of Kings Mountain
- 1781—Drafted for 3 months. Discharged by Isaac Shelby

Other members of the Crockett clan also served the community in various capacities. Joseph Crockett, John's brother and Davy's uncle, had his arm broken by a rifle ball in the Indian attack that killed David's grandparents. Having lost the use of his hand, Joseph "fashioned an imitation hand so that he could eat."[74] Joseph was appointed by the first territorial governor of Tennessee, William Blount, as the "straymaster" for Sullivan County.[75] Straymasters were charged with gathering up stray animals and ensuring return to their rightful owners. The position was not considered strenuous and was often awarded to veterans who had suffered debilitating war wounds.

---

73 Pension application of Robert Crockett, S30353, Southern Campaigns American Revolution Pension Statements and Rosters, https://revwarapps.org/s30353.pdf, accessed March 11, 2021.

74 Jones, *Crockett Cousins*, 80.

75 William Blount, *The Blount Journal, 1790-1796* (Knoxville, The University of Tennessee Press, 1955), 33.

Crocketts at Kings Mountain

In the "Roster of Soldiers from North Carolina in the American Revolution," Crockett's father John was listed as a member of the Lincoln County militia.[76] He served as a volunteer soldier under the command of Col. Isaac Shelby at the Battle of Kings Mountain, which was a pivotal engagement in the southern campaign of the American Revolution. British Major Patrick Ferguson (1744–1780), under the command of General Charles Cornwallis (1738–1805), had recruited and trained about one thousand loyalists, or "Tories," from the New York and New Jersey area and had sailed to Charleston, South Carolina. Wataugan rangers had been harassing British units in the south, handing them a defeat at Musgrove's Mill. To those "over-mountain men" (frontiersmen from outposts "over the mountains" west of the Appalachians), Major Ferguson sent word that if they continued to resist English authority and harass the British army in skirmishes along the mountain border, he would "march his army over the mountains, hang their leaders, and lay their country waste with fire and sword."

Unfortunately for the British, the message got through to the predominantly Ulster-Scots settlements. Ferguson's bluster and bellicosity had the opposite effect from what he intended, serving only to stoke the frontiersmen's fire and determination. While the overmountain settlers took Ferguson's threat seriously, they were not inclined to submit to his threats. Rather than wait for Ferguson to bring his army to them, the overmountain men brought the fight to Ferguson, who had established a headquarters on the fringe of the western frontier at Gilbert Town, North Carolina.

Overmountain militias from the hilly frontier areas of Tennessee, Virginia, and North Carolina joined together—composed in the main of Ulster-Scots settlers. This combined force grew to well over a

---

76   North Carolina Daughters of the American Revolution, *Roster of Soldiers from North Carolina in the American Revolution* (Baltimore: Genealogical Publishing Company, 1967), 480.

thousand, and pursued Ferguson to Kings Mountain in South Carolina (near the North Carolina line just west of Charlotte), where Ferguson determined to make a stand. His combined forces of Tory (British loyalist) soldiers from New York, New Jersey, and the Carolinas totaled approximately eleven hundred men.

Ferguson, a Highland Scot, was a courageous, well-trained, experienced, and capable officer on a site well-suited for an effective defense. The numbers of combatants on each side were evenly matched. The British forces should have had the upper hand, having picked their defensive site, with adequate time to fortify. However, Ferguson's fatal miscalculation was in underestimating the abilities of these "back water men ... a set of mongrels," as he termed them. His British conceit had been bolstered by recent victories over colonial militias in the Carolinas.

In his conceit, Ferguson, with time in abundance, did not bother to build breastworks, even though timber was plentiful at the site. Adequately constructed fixed defenses on high ground could have shielded his troops from the deadly fire of the militiamen. Ferguson was clearly unprepared for the fierce onslaught of these seasoned fighters.

Around noon on October 7, 1780, as the British forces occupied the high ground of Kings Mountain, they found themselves surrounded by a force of well over a thousand overmountain militia. Given the conditions, terrain, and lack of British breastworks, the superior range and accuracy of the overmountain men's rifled long guns proved to be a significant advantage over shorter-range, less-accurate, smooth-bored muskets used by the British and Tories, who were arrayed in conventional lines of battle atop the steep, hog-backed ridge.

Robert Young from Greene County, Tennessee, was credited with having fired the first shot, that hit the mounted Patrick Ferguson (who was subsequently hit with several other shots). Young had named his rifle "Sweet Lips" in honor of his wife, Mary Douglas Young. The rifle, a typical .40-caliber early Pennsylvania-Kentucky style rifle signed

"Gor Dunkin," is now on display at the Tennessee State Museum in Nashville.

The hour-long battle that ensued was dominated by the accurate and withering fire of the frontier riflemen, who employed their long guns from behind the cover of rocks and trees. Their marksmanship proved deadly and effective against British force. These frontier Scots were quickly establishing a reputation as excellent marksmen and effective fighters—a reputation that David Crockett, as the son of one of the heroes of that battle, would later take to a legendary level.

The result was a decisive defeat of the British force, and a victory for the overmountain men. The British major Patrick Ferguson was killed, along with 224 of his men. A total of 163 British and Tories were wounded and 716 taken prisoner. The loss to revolutionary forces was comparatively low, with 28 killed and 62 wounded. The lopsided toll of the battle, combined with the loss of Ferguson and his entire command, changed the complexion of the war in the south. British General Charles Cornwallis had lost his finest officer in Major Ferguson, as well as a thousand of his troops, being bested by a ragtag rabble of militia whom he would not have even considered an organized fighting unit. This devastating defeat caused Cornwallis to reconsider his southern strategy of recruiting southern loyalists and marching them northward to meet up and support loyalist and British forces in Virginia. Subsequent defeats handed to the British at Cowpens and Guilford Court House were enough to cause Cornwallis to return to Virginia by sea.

Significance of the Victory at Kings Mountain

The importance of the Battle of Kings Mountain was twofold: it was a much-needed southern victory for the patriots after a number of embarrassing defeats in the south. The Kings Mountain victory halted what had been a successful advance of Cornwallis into the heart of the Carolinas. In the northeast, General Washington was thus given time to oust the ineffective General Horatio Gates, replacing him with

General Nathanael Greene, who would prove effective in repelling later British advances.

After American victory in 1783, soldiers of the Continental Line were entitled to land in return for their service in the American army. For his service, Nathanael Greene received vast parcels of overmountain land (which he never occupied) and was honored by having a Tennessee county named for him: Greene County—the county of David Crockett's birth.

The overmountain riflemen had proven their worth. For many of them, the Ulster-Scots in particular, the fighting had given them a chance to settle long-simmering scores with the British. The ancestors of these militiamen had faced British abuse and oppression in the old countries of Ireland and Scotland. Here on the American frontier, where their fathers and grandfathers had run to escape generations of economic, religious, political, and social oppression, they were able to make the most of their opportunity to strike back at their long-time oppressors.

The American victory at Kings Mountain was testament to the tough resourcefulness of the Ulster-Scots volunteers and the deadly accuracy of their long rifles. Some thirty years later, descendants of many of these men would use these same skills at the Battle of New Orleans—with similar effective results. The accuracy of the rifle fire and the frontier toughness of the overmountain men, together with sound and capable leadership from a group of determined militia officers, were the keys to success in this pivotal Revolutionary War battle.

Events that took place after the British surrender tarnished the overall success of the campaign. Being relatively untrained in the rules of war, as they were at the time, there was not a good understanding of the "white flag of surrender." A number of Tories and British were killed after the flag of surrender had been raised, and some killed after they had laid down their weapons. In addition, the day before prisoners were to be turned over to the American regular army custody, militia members held a "trial," in which captives were "convicted" for crimes against the general population and were hung for those alleged offenses. These actions were clearly beyond the authority of these overmountain militia members.

See Appendix C for a listing of some of the men who fought at Kings Mountain and who would have been familiar with the Crocketts.

CHAPTER 7:

Horse Camp Creek and the Mill Disaster in Greene County

The site near the Nolichucky River where David had been born offered protection because of its close proximity to Fort Lee, which was across the river on a hill overlooking the settlement. When the John Crockett family left Strong Springs near the Nolichucky River around 1792 when David was about six, they resettled less than ten miles from there in an area called "Horse Camp Creek," known today as Walkertown in northeastern Tennessee. In this Greene County neighborhood, the Crocketts joined the growing vanguard of settlers continuing to move into this area about three miles northwest of Quaker Knobs. Heavy settlement activity was occurring in Greene County during this period, due in part to diminishing threats from Native American tribes.

In his *Narrative*, David described the family's move, saying they took up residence near Joseph Hawkins (Rebecca Hawkins Crockett's brother and David's uncle): "Shortly after this, my father removed, and settled in the same county, about ten miles above Greenville" [*N*, 20]. John Crockett had obtained land in this neighborhood from the

State of North Carolina with a 1792 survey calling for "197 acres on Stockton's Fork of Lick Creek."[77] The deed for his tract also described "the horse fork of Lick Creek," "the head of McCartney's Creek," and "Horse Camp Creek." At the time the Crocketts lived in this neighborhood, it would have been known as the "headwaters of the Horse Camp Creek," one of several tributaries of Lick Creek. These Greene County waterways should not be confused with "Horse Creek" or "Camp Creek" as they were known at the time, both of which also drained into the Nolichucky River.

Regardless, when searching maps of Greene County (ten miles north of Greeneville), we do not find "a Stockton's Fork of Lick Creek," nor several of the other water features listed in the Crockett land deed. It was not unusual for the names of terrain features (or even entire towns) to change over time. While this writer is unaware of any publication that identifies the exact location of the Crockett family home plot, the Crockett property was settled somewhere within the boundaries of four creek tributaries, presumably with Stockton's Fork being the primary artery within the Crockett acreage.

The Greene County area in which John Crockett and his family settled encompassed today's neighborhoods of Walkertown, Newmansville, and Union Temple. Lick Creek and its tributaries occupy a wide area that winds a circuitous path and empties into the Nolichucky River at what is known as the "Bend of the Chucky." This watershed provided fertile bottom soil, offering the kind of prime farming land that attracted settlers eager for agricultural prosperity.

Web of Community Revealed by Property Records

When trying to reconstruct the character of the people in a historic neighborhood, it's useful to identify as many names of residents as possible. With land acquisition taking place at an increasing pace as

---

77   Greene County Deed Book Vol 3, Page 320, 27 Nov 1792, John Crockett from St of NC 197 acres Stogdons Fork, Lick Creek. Grant #1243.

land was being divided, granted, and sold for personal use and for profit-driven land speculation, an enormous amount of documentation was created by county officials and clerks. This deed and grant paperwork was created to record the establishment of boundaries and ownership, to legitimize homestead claims, and to justify fees and payments to government agencies. In addition to their role in documenting and establishing land claims in the 1790s, these types of legal documentation offer rich and fertile archives of material that can help establish the history of a region, tell stories through the names of families who lived on the land, and support other historical resources like census records, militia muster rolls, or tax records.

As such, the names of property owners listed on official deeds in the Horse Camp Creek area of 1790s Greene County reflected a rich variety of names of English, Scots-Irish, and German families, including those of Robert Wilson, Robert Blackburn, John Gass, Charles Arrington, James Jones, Joseph Hacker, John Tye, John Gillehan, John Dodd, Abraham Hayes, and Andrew Patterson.[78] Horse Camp Creek must have been a colorful and diverse settlement of pioneers, equally unafraid to risk their capital, their lives, and the safety of their families in the hopes of carving out a better life on the frontier, regardless of the country of origin of their forebears.

Other useful tools in understanding the composition of historic neighborhoods are the public records that list residents who witnessed the official documents of others. "Deed witnesses" were most often neighbors brought in because of their proximity and convenience (assuming that one neighbor would ask another neighbor to sign as a witness), and familiarity (neighbors who witnessed deeds would know each other well and trust each other's word).

Many examples exist of neighbors witnessing legal transactions for each other. On October 20, 1787, Joseph Ray received a deed that described his property as being "in Greene County on head of

---

78   NC Grants in Greene County, Grant#/Page #: #58/351-354; #337/230; 652; 51; #521/300; #1263/316; #385/4; #385/4; #58/351-354;#1910/87; #1910/87; #1910/87.

McCartney's Creek, adjoining John Crockett's property." In 1789, John Crockett witnessed a deed from Henry Cross to Thomas Pierce.[79] During this period in 1793, Henry Cross procured land on the "Sinking Fork of Lick Creek," on a parcel adjoining land owned by Shadrach and Drew Morris.[80] Thomas Pierce had bought land from Gideon Morris on a branch of Lick Creek in February 1787, which was documented with a deed witnessed by John Newman and Nineon Steel.[81]

David's uncle Joseph Hawkins had a land grant that called for 200 acres on the headwaters of the Horse Stamp [sic Camp] Fork of Lick Creek.[82] The land occupied by Absalom Stonecipher had been deeded to his father Henry Stonecipher on the "West fork of Lick Creek on Joseph Hawkins' [David's uncle] ... conditional line between Isaac Odle and Joseph Henderson."[83]

In 1783, Isaac Odle had been granted three hundred acres on a branch of Lick Creek adjoining Joseph Henderson and John Newman.[84] Samuel Humberd received a 1791 land grant "on Lick Creek adjoining his land, adjoining Samuel Cotter and Thomas Ray."[85] Stephen Cotter had land adjoining Joseph Hawkins and Robert Wilson, received in

---

79   NC Grant #396, 392.

80   Grant #1220, 329 29 July 1793, 200 acres on Sinking Creek Fork of Lick Creek adj Drew Morris and Shadrach Morris.

81   8 Feb 1787—p. 12. Gideon Morris to Thomas Pierce—99 Acres on a branch of Lick Creek—Witness, John Newman & Nineon Steel. NC Land Grants Recorded in Greene County, Southern Historical Press, 1981.

82   NC Land Grants in Greene Co—p. 140, Grant #831, to Joseph Hawkins—200 acres on headwaters of Horse Stamp [sic. Camp] Fork of Lick Creek.

83   Henry Stonesifer—Father of Absalom. 6 May 1796, Book ___ Page 26, 150 acres on West fork of Lick Creek, from Rudolph Bough [sic. Bugh?] ... Joseph Hawkins line ... conditional line between Isaac Odle & Jos Henderson. Witness: Jacob Jurat[?] and John Jones.

84   NC Grant #385, p. 4, 13 Oct 1783, to Isaac Odle, 300 Acres in Washington County on a branch of Lick Creek adjoining Joseph Henderson, John Newman, John Tye, and Joseph Hacker.

85   NC Grant #910, p. 379, 26 Dec 1791, to Samuel Humber, 50 acres on Lick Creek adjoining his land, Samuel Cotter and Thomas Ray.

1791 on "Horse Camp Creek."[86] In 1782, Robert Wilson received "239 acres on headwaters of Horse Camp Creek." [87, 88]

An examination of the records shows that in March 1785, William Stockton of Greene County conveyed three hundred acres to Dutton Lane.[89] Phillip Babb received one hundred acres on the "south branch of Lick Creek, adjoining William Stockton."[90] The Babb name has continued to be used in this area: "Babb's Mill Road" cuts right across John Crockett's old tract, with many of these creeks and streams terminating at Walkertown.

This examination of property deeds and grants provides more than just a litany or listing of property owners and legal witnesses. These records show not only who owned and lived on the land in 1790s Greene County, but also gives some insight into the web of relationships among the families living in that early region of northeastern Tennessee. The John Crockett family was part of this web, along with young David Crockett and his siblings.

The Story of Absalom Stonecipher's Shooting

One family in this Greene County web of community with whom the Crocketts interacted was the Stonecipher family. The Stoneciphers had been stone cutters in Bohemia, Westphalia, and finally Eiserfeld, Germany, for many centuries—a profession that came to be reflected in the family surname. Arriving as immigrants in Virginia aboard the ship *Johannes* from Rotterdam in 1749, the Stoneciphers came with

---

86   NC Grant #821, p. 141, 13 Feb 1791, to Stephen Cotter, 100 acres on Horse Camp Creek of Lick Creek adjoining Robert Wilson and Joseph Hawkins.

87   NC Grants in Greene County, Grant#/Page #: #58/351-354; #337/230; #521/300; #1263/316; #385/4; #385/4; #58/351-354;#1910/87; #1910/87; #1910/87.

88   NC Grant #58, p. 351-354, 23 Oct 1782, to Robert Wilson 239 acres on headwaters of Horse Camp Creek. Adjoins John Gillehan.

89   11 March 1785, Wm Stockton of Greene County, NC, to Dutton Lane, 300 Acres granted to Wm Stockton by the State of NC, Attest John Gass and Wm Hughes.

90   St of NC Grant #521, p. 300, Phillip Babb 100 acres in Greene County.

a practiced skill at stonecutting and were employed in the iron works at Culpepper, Virginia. John Henry and his wife Henricas Stonecipher left Virginia in 1777 and moved to Tennessee.

In his *Narrative*, David Crockett tells a story of an incident that occurred at the Stoneciphers' homestead in Greene County, sometime between 1787 and 1796:

> There another circumstance happened, which made a lasting impression on my memory, though I was still a small child. Joseph Hawkins, who was a brother to my mother, was hunting in the woods for deer. He was passing near a thicket of brush, in which one of our neighbors was gathering some grapes, as it was in the fall of the year, and the grape season. The body of the man was hidden by the brush, and it was only as he would raise his hand to pull the bunches, that any part of him could be seen. It was a likely place for a deer; and my uncle, having no suspicion that it was any human being, but supposing the raising of the hand to be the occasional twitch of a deer's ear, fired at the lump, and as the devil would have it, unfortunately shot the man through the body. I saw my father draw a silk handkerchief through the bullet hole, and entirely through his body; yet after a while he got well as any one would have thought it. What become of him, or whether he is dead or alive, I don't know; but I reckon he did'ent fancy the business of gathering grapes in an out-of-the-way thicket soon again. [*N*, 20–21]

Crockett's sense of humor was readily apparent in this passage from his *Narrative*. The grape-picker shot by Joseph Hawkins was their neighbor, Absalom Stonecipher, who was taken to the home of Samuel Humberd, his house boasting a tall limestone fireplace and chimney. David's father John was sent for and asked to treat the gunshot Stonecipher. It's reasonable to assume that Stonecipher may have been placed in front of that fireplace in preparation for treatment, and that John Crockett may have heated up a poker or other implements to stanch the bleeding from Stonecipher's wounds.

Site of the Samuel Humberd Home with original chimney built around 1782.

Etched into the rock on the right side of the fireplace the initials for Samuel Humberd: "S[inverted] H Oct. 9, 1782."

Absalom Stonecipher, then about age 25, was nursed back to health in that house by Samuel Humbert's daughter, Sarah. Her nursing skills must have been superb, for Stonecipher later married her on March 10, 1796. Absalom and Sarah Humberd Stonecipher went on to have ten children. The house later came into their possession. Absalom Stonecipher died at the ripe old age of 82, which was not bad for a man shot through the body at a time when there were no hospitals, no doctors, and little medicine.

At the time David recounted this tale in 1834, Stonecipher was indeed alive and still living in the old neighborhood where he would continue to live until 1851, some fifteen years after David's own death at the Alamo. Both Absalom and Sarah Stonecipher are buried in marked graves in the Babb Valley Cemetery in Greene County.[91]

The Stonecipher house is located about a mile south of the junction of Kingsport Highway (93) and Rheatown Road (351) in the Walkertown community. Adjacent to the Stonecipher house is a sizeable spring that feeds into Newmansville Creek. The home on the site today maintains the original stone chimney dating to the 1780s, although the original house structure has been replaced or added on to.

The Crockett Mill Disaster at Cove Creek

John Crockett had sold his property around Lick Creek, the proceeds of which he likely used to partner with a prominent Greene County resident to build a water-powered mill along Cove Creek. David Crockett wrote in his *Narrative* of these Greene County events occurring around 1794, when he was seven or eight years old:

> The next move that my father made was to the mouth of Cove Creek, where he and a man by the name of Thomas Gilbreath [*sic*] undertook to build a mill in partnership. [*N*, 21–22]

Crockett's partner was Thomas Galbraith (last name sometimes found spelled as "Gilbreath"), a prominent citizen of early Greene and Jefferson Counties, and thus an able and qualified partner for John Crockett.

Thomas Galbraith was born in 1751 in Bucks County, Pennsylvania, making him close in age to John Crockett. Galbraith served in the Revolutionary War in Captain Abraham Miller's and Charles Craig's Companies from June 10, 1775, to July 1, 1776. He was involved in a skirmish at Lechmere Point, which earned him a pension (determined from his application made June 10, 1818). On May 30, 1779, Galbraith

---

91   From Arless Stonecipher—Indiana State Univ.—Mertin Genealogy Letter.

married Elizabeth Hayes, daughter of Nicholas Hayes, in Bedford County, Virginia. Nicholas Hayes later moved from Virginia to Greene County, Tennessee (as did his daughter and son-in-law Galbraith), and owned property adjoining John Crockett's at Walkertown, further establishing a Galbraith-Crockett connection.

As a partner to John Crockett in their Cove Creek mill partnership, Galbraith proved to be a skilled and competent millwright. They placed the location of this water-powered mill at the mouth of Cove Creek where it empties into the Nolichucky River near the old community of Dulaney (what was later called Filler's Mill). The closest town to the mill site was Greeneville, about ten miles distant.

The elevation at the mouth of Cove Creek is approximately twelve hundred feet above sea level. But only four miles away heading into the mountains toward Hot Springs, the elevation at Chucky Mountain climbs to over three thousand feet. The proximity to these mountains and the steep fall of the creek proved a factor in the disaster that would soon occur.

When the Crockett-Galbraith mill was almost completed, a heavy rainstorm passed through the county. With torrential waters cascading down from the high mountains to the east, feeding both the Nolichucky River and Cove Creek, the river and creek both quickly rose and overflowed their banks. Both Crockett's home and the nearly completed mill were completely washed out by flood waters. David Crockett recollected in his *Narrative*:

> They went on very well with their work until it was nigh done, when there came the second epistle to Noah's fresh [flood], and away went their mill, shot, lock, and barrel. I remember the water rose so high, that it got up into the house we lived in, and my father moved us out of it, to keep us from being drowned. I was now about seven or eight years old, and have a pretty distinct recollection of every thing that was going on. From his bad luck in that business, and being ready to wash out from mill building, my father

again removed, and this time settled in Jefferson county, now in the state of Tennessee; where he opened a tavern on the road from Abbingdon to Knoxville. [*N*, 21]

Losing both his home and the mill was a heavy financial blow to John Crockett, who had invested—and now lost—the money from the sale of his 197 acres at Lick Creek.

Some relics from the ruined Crockett mill remained. According to a Greene County source, the two mated Crockett millstones were on display on opposite sides of the road approaching the town of Dulaney for many years. Another source reported that a road grader broke one of the stones, and that the pieces were in the possession of a Phillip Rader, who was said to have bought the millstones in 1945: "These stones had been used in the old Crockett Mill, which had stood just below the old Fillers Mill."[92]

A millstone said to have been from Crockett's mill was given to the Crockett Tavern and Historic Site in Morristown, where it may still be seen today. This millstone has obviously been broken and carefully put back together, with a steel ring around the circumference of the stone to hold the pieces together. This would bolster the claim that it was one of the two stones found near the site of John Crockett's mill.

While the floodwaters of Cove Creek and the Nolichucky washed away Crockett's investment and dissolved his mill partnership with Thomas Galbraith, the two families nevertheless remained close. Members of the Galbraith family were said to have been present at the wedding of David and Polly Finley in 1806.[93] Galbraith's association with John Crockett may have gone beyond the ill-fated mill venture. Historical material published by the Crockett Tavern Historic Site suggests that John Crockett lived for a time in a house owned

---

92   Direct Descendants of David Crockett Publication, February 2015.

93   James Paul Galbraith, "Galbraith Ancestry" (Knoxville, TN, undated genealogical paper). Corroborated by Mrs. Foy Quarels. From the papers of Miss Lurana Franklin—a resident of the area of Dumplin Valley and descendent of the Galbraiths.

by Galbraith after the mill disaster.[94] This information also appears in the Whittenburg and Torrence genealogy book on Crockett, which surmises: "Following this disaster, [the Crocketts] moved to the cabin of his friend, Thomas Galbraith, who took them in until a new location was found in Jefferson County, where he built a log inn or tavern, eight miles East of Dandridge, on the road running from Abingdon, Virginia, to Knoxville."[95] (The associations seem right here except that the tavern was located on the same road, but just northeast of Morristown and not near Jefferson City/Mossy Creek.) It is also possible that Galbraith later helped Crockett acquire a rented facility that became John Crockett's stockman's hostelry.

Nicholas Hayes, father-in-law of Thomas Galbraith, eventually operated the Hayes ferry on the French Broad River five miles east of Dandridge. The ferry was located at what people today know as Swann's Bridge, adjacent to the Interstate 40 bridge over the French Broad River east of Dandridge.[96] Nicholas Hayes signed the "Petition of the Inhabitants of the Western Country" in 1784.[97]

Thomas and Elizabeth Galbraith later migrated to Jefferson County (as did the Crocketts; see the following chapter), finally settling one mile west of Dandridge at Branner's Mill.[98] A great-grandson of Thomas Galbraith—Dr. James D. Hoskins—was a native of Dandridge and later became the distinguished president of the University of Tennessee from 1933–1946.[99]

The Cove Creek mill disaster appears to have been a crushing blow from which John Crockett never fully recovered. In the years 1794 to

---

94   Crockett Tavern and Pioneer Museum pamphlet.

95   Torrence and Whittenburg, *Colonel "Davy" Crockett*, 4.

96   The Bicentennial Committee of Jefferson County, Tennessee, *Heritage* (Jefferson County, 1976), 9.

97   Petition of the Inhabitants of the Western Country, TnGenWeb Project website. https://www.tngenweb.org/pre1796/178712f.html. Accessed 18 March 2021.

98   Galbraith, "Galbraith Ancestry," 63.

99   Galbraith, "Galbraith Ancestry," 73.

1795, even with the help of Galbraith, John apparently liquidated all his property, some of it perhaps not voluntarily, and moved his family to the rented home in Jefferson County where he ran a tavern for wagoners and traveling stockmen [*N*, 22]. See the following chapter on Jefferson County.

Today, the site of the washed-out Crockett mill is on private property, with no public roads passing by it. A float trip down the Nolichucky River will pass by it on the right bank heading downstream. A Tennessee state historical marker is located near the Cove Creek mill site at the intersection of the South Allen's Bridge road and the West Allen's Bridge road (where the Allen's Bridge crosses the Nolichucky River in the south of Greene County). From the Allen's Bridge, it is 1.3 miles up the river to get to the mouth of Cove Creek. Or take the Asheville Highway out of Greeneville heading south on state highway 107/70 to Filler's Mill Road. Turn right and watch for the bridge over Cove Creek. If a person put a boat in the river at the Davy Crockett dam, it is 2.4 miles downstream to the mouth of Cove Creek.

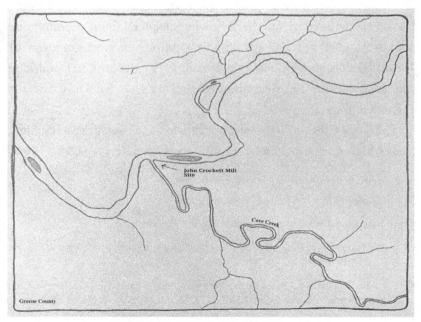

Mouth of Cove Creek, Nolichucky River, 2019. Henry Susong (May 2013), owner of the site at the mouth of Cove Creek.

The Recovery of Uncle James "Dumb Jimmie" Crockett

A Crockett kidnapping that occurred nearly twenty years prior would come to be resolved, largely with the assistance of friends and associates of John Crockett in Greene County. Back in 1777, a combined attack by Creek and Cherokee Indians had killed Davy's grandparents near Rogersville, Tennessee [N, 16]. In this attack, John Crockett's brother, James "Jimmie" Crockett, was taken prisoner by the Cherokee. James Crockett could neither hear nor speak and was thus referred to often as "dumb Jimmie." According to David, his Uncle Jimmie "… remained with [the Indians] for 17 years and 9 months when he was discovered and recollected by my father and his eldest brother, William Crockett; and was purchased back by them from an Indian Trader" [N, 16]. Held for over 17 years, Jimmie Crockett's return to his family would have occurred in 1795.

The "Indian Trader" who helped William and John Crockett buy back their brother may have been Isaac Thomas. In July 1793, Isaac Thomas was granted land on "Starkton's [sic Stockton's] Mill Creek, a branch of Lick Creek, adjoining Dutton Lane and John Morris." Isaac Thomas was a neighbor to John Crockett.[100] Thomas was a trader among the Cherokees and acted as the pilot in 1776 for Col. William Christian's campaign against the Overhill Cherokee Indian Towns.[101] Isaac Thomas's relationship as a trader among the Cherokee may have provided some help in being able to "purchase" Jimmie back from the tribe.

Two other traders with the Cherokees in the Watauga region were Andrew Greer and Caesar Dugger. Andrew Greer became the first merchant in Greeneville. Both men were prominent settlers on the Watauga and Nolichucky. The Crocketts would have known Dugger and Greer and it is possible that the two traders could have had a hand in the recovery of Jimmie.[102]

---

100   NC Grant #1263, p. 374, 29 July 1793.

101   Ramsey, *Annals of Tennessee*, 166.

102   Richard Doughty, *Greeneville: One Hundred Year Portrait (1775–1875)*, 1975.

Another connection to the Cherokee, which may have helped in Jimmie's recovery, could have been Dudley Cox, an early resident of Jefferson County, who continued to have close ties to the Cherokees up until his death around 1812. One of the many Cherokees with whom Cox associated was Chief John Ross, who worked with the White settlers and the US government to try to retain lands claimed by the Cherokees. Chief Ross's efforts for the Cherokees were in vain, however, due on one hand to Andrew Jackson's double-dealing and on the other hand to White settlers who, like Jackson, had no regard for any promises made to the Cherokees regarding rights to their land. Cox may have known the Crocketts from Jefferson County and may have provided some influence in procuring Jimmie's repatriation.

By the time James was found and returned to his family, John Crockett had already moved out of Greene County and into Jefferson County where he would establish a tavern on the main Holston road. The ability of an "Indian Trader" (as recounted in David Crockett's *Narrative*) to help John and William Crockett "purchase back" their brother from the Cherokee, may have had assistance from Greene County friends and associates, or as a result of information carried by travelers who frequented Crockett's tavern in Jefferson County, Tennessee.

CHAPTER 8:

Early Jefferson County and John Crockett's Tavern

The ill-fated mill venture at Cove Creek in Greene County must have been a turning point in John Crockett's life. After the 1794 flood that destroyed his cabin and mill, John Crockett moved his family southwest to Jefferson County (present-day Hamblen County). This move came at a time when David says he was "about seven or eight" [*N*, 21].

John had likely invested all his available assets in the Cove Creek mill—and had to watch all of it wash away in the flood. David wrote in his *Narrative* about the family's state of affairs at that time: "I began to make my acquaintance with hard times, and a plenty of them." He added: "My father again removed, and this time settled in Jefferson County, now in the state of Tennessee; where he opened a tavern on the road from Abingdon to Knoxville" [*N*, 22]. The hard circumstances faced by the Crockett family may well have contributed to increased alcohol consumption on the part of John Crockett.

The State of North Carolina provided Jefferson County land grants to Revolutionary War veterans living in Washington and Greene

Counties. While John Crockett would not have been entitled to a direct grant because he was not a soldier of North Carolina Continental Line, he had received two payments for his service (Kings Mountain), which qualified him to make an application for land near Mossy Creek in Jefferson County. He purchased this Mossy Creek land at the rate of fifty shillings per one hundred acres (paid to the North Carolina treasury).

John Crockett's grant from the State of North Carolina on May 27, 1792, called for "300 acres South Side of the Main Holston Road within a few miles of Perkins' Iron Works on Mossy Creek and the waters of the Holston River."[103] John acquired this land by Grant #1050, dated the 14th of April 1792.[104] The Mossy Creek neighborhood was an early center of economic activity within Jefferson County. While the creek was only about five miles in length, the water fell at a rapid rate and thus provided a robust flow that attracted grist mills, sawmills, and other manufacturers that relied on waterpower.

James Shackford described Crockett's Mossy Creek tavern site on land at the junction of the Knoxville to Abingdon Road, near the ironworks (the present site of Jefferson City). He supposed that this was the only site at which Crockett ran a tavern (a remaining point of historical debate):

> Another tract which John bought on April 24, 1792, was evidently David's home place during his early years after 1794, and therefore has a peculiar interest for us: Three hundred acres lying on Mossy Creek in Jefferson County. The Crocketts did not move to it until after the disaster to the Cove Creek Mill in 1794. Its sale on November 4, 1795, under the sheriff's hammer, reveals John's failure to escape debt. The father either remained in possession of a

---

103   Jefferson County Deed Book 3, p. 289.

104   Jefferson Co Deed record Book *CD*, 1792–1799, pp. 159–60, Item 89, later transferred to deed book "Q," 1797–1802, pp. 94–95 with errors in the transference.

remnant of these acres or perhaps continued to live there in the employ of the purchaser. Certainly it was here that he built the tavern David describes in the Autobiography, so that David continued to live there for several more years.[105]

John Crockett indeed owned the land for three years and four months. As Shackford noted, the sheriff sold Crockett's land on November 4, 1795, presumably for unpaid taxes or debts. The land was purchased by William Line[106] (who later sold the property on May 17, 1804, to Henry Howell of Grainger County).[107]

By late 1795, the Crocketts had taken up use of a cabin belonging to Thomas Galbraith, John's friend and partner in their ruined Cove Creek mill venture. John Crockett would later rent a log tavern and inn about eight miles east of Dandridge, also on the road running from Abingdon, Virginia, to Knoxville, Tennessee.

The actual location of David Crockett's Jefferson County boyhood home has been long debated. Three locations have been postulated over the past hundred years. In his 1956 book, James B. Shackford noted Mossy Creek (Jefferson City) as the site. As early as 1902, a location eight miles east of Dandridge was given as the location of the Crockett family home plot. Later, a Tennessee Historical Commission marker in the Morristown/Russellville area indicated its estimation of the location of John Crockett's tavern.

Shackford was in error when he wrote: "Early maps show that prior to 1800 there was only one road running through the county to Washington, DC—the Main Holston Road. Not until 1814 do maps record a second road running south through Dandridge, turning east

105   Shackford, *David Crockett: The Man and the Legend*, 6.

106   Jefferson County Deed Book Q, p. 94–95.

107   Jefferson County Deed Book G, p. 65.

and then north and coming into the earlier road around the Virginia line."[108]

Shackford may not have had complete information. It happens that another early road from Abingdon was likely the one running south of Bays Mountain through Dandridge. The road that went through Mossy Creek followed one of the many buffalo traces and game trails that ran from the Eastern Seaboard, originating from a time well before men began to use it. The route through Mossy Creek (today Jefferson City) is more direct when heading to Knoxville from Abingdon and Greeneville.

As mentioned by Shackford, John Crockett later lost title to this Mossy Creek land in Jefferson County. Stanley Folmsbee, in his article, "The Early Career of David Crockett," noted: "It is probable, since John Crockett lost title to the Mossy Creek land, that he later moved to the Morristown site and operated there the tavern which David mentioned in his Autobiography." Both the Sons of the American Revolution and the Tennessee Historical Commission have confirmed and marked the site of the John Crockett Tavern at Morristown.

For the next sixteen years, Jefferson County would be home to David, then age nine. The young Crockett would live in Jefferson County longer than he would in any other spot in Tennessee, later living five years in Franklin County from 1812–1817; four years in Lawrence County from 1818–1822; and twelve years in Gibson County from 1823–1835 (less the time he lived in Washington when working as a Tennessee congressman).

Background and History of Jefferson/Hamblen County

Early Jefferson County encompassed most of what is today Hamblen County, as well as parts of Cocke and Sevier Counties. Set in northeast Tennessee, Jefferson County was bounded on the north by the Holston River, running from northeast to southwest. On the south, the county

---

108   Shackford, *David Crockett: The Man and the Legend*, 294.

was bounded by the Nolichucky River, the French Broad River, and the English Mountains. A chain of Appalachian ridges known as Bays Mountain runs northeast to southwest through the center of Jefferson County.

Fresh water was abundant in the area, flowing from cold springs along both sides of Bays Mountain. These springs fed the two primary creeks in the county: Long Creek and Dumplin Creek, the headwaters of each rising at about the same point on either side of Bays Mountain near Finley Gap, and flowing in opposite directions.

Land surveying began in the area during the 1770s, with the first permanent settlers beginning to arrive in the early 1780s. Gideon, Absolem, and Daniel Morriss were some of the earliest, settling around 1783 near what is today Morristown. Around the same year, other early settlers began establishing homesteads on the headwaters of Long Creek near Finley Gap, including Samuel Lyle, James McCuistion, Jeremiah Nicholson, John Jacobs, and John Blackburn. Other homesteads on the headwaters of Dumplin Creek were those of Samuel Rankin, Thomas and Richard Rankin, John and William Bradshaw, William Bettis, and William Finley.[109] The Finley Gap neighborhood (taking its name from the Finley family) would later be the location of the first home of David Crockett and wife Polly Finley.

The Great Indian War Trail and Early Jefferson County Roads

The "Great Indian War Trail" enters Jefferson County just north of Bull's Gap and proceeds along the south ridge of Bays Mountain, north of the Nolichucky and French Broad Rivers. It crosses the headwaters of Long Creek near Finley Gap, and leaves the county near the community of Dumplin. The Great Indian War Trail passes close to

---

109   W. A. Challacombe, *The Benjamin Blackburn Family and Notes on Blackburns in America* (Carlinville, IL, 1942), repr, Mason, MI: Robert and Betty Peebles, 1988, 62.

what is today Sam Martin Road; a landmark rock that stood beside the war trail is still identifiable.[110]

As one of the earliest thoroughfares within Jefferson County, Bull's Gap Road followed Dumplin Creek by Flat Gap north of Dandridge, and on into Sevier County through the Dumplin community. This early road and commerce route would have fed the populations of early communities that sprang up on Long Creek and Dumplin Creek.

This ancient war trail that traversed Jefferson County was also used by American troops during the Revolutionary War. In 1776, Colonel William Christian led about eighteen hundred men on a campaign against Cherokees who had allied with the British. Christian's route to engage the Cherokees took him from a rendezvous point at the Great Island of the Holston (in the Watauga area of northeast Tennessee), down through what is today Greene County, along Lick Creek to the Nolichucky River, and then down Long Creek in Jefferson County. According to Ramsey's *The Annals of Tennessee*:

> Isaac Thomas, a trader among the Cherokees, acted as pilot. He conducted the army along a narrow but plain war path up Long Creek to its source, and down Dumplin Creek to a point a few miles from its mouth.[111]

Colonel Christian's route with his eighteen hundred men followed the War Trail and took them along the length of what was to become Jefferson County—from Bull's Gap in the northeast to Dumplin in the southwest. This expedition was the first time many of these soldiers had seen eastern Tennessee, and the landscape's beauty would draw many of them back to settle in the area after the war's conclusion. It is not known precisely who was on this military campaign, but it is known that many of them later became the earliest settlers of the area.

---

110   "Standing Rock on the War Path" reference in Thomas and David McCuistion Deed.

111   Ramsey, *Annals of Tennessee*.

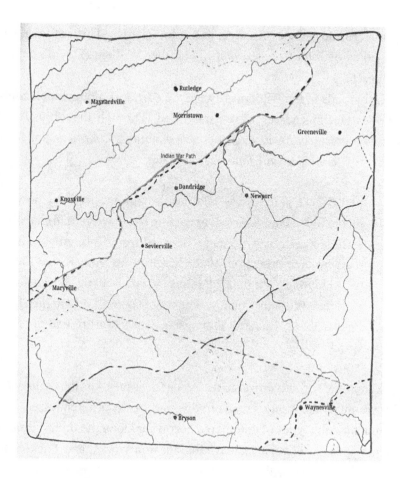

Samuel Lyle is said to have been in the group and settled on property situated on the War Trail at the headwaters of Long Creek.[112]

A number of the men were known to have been militia soldiers and rangers during Revolutionary War battles in the Carolinas. A few names of early Jefferson County settlers who were military veterans included Alexander Outlaw, John Blackburn, Thomas McCuistion, James Scott, Richard Rankin and Samuel Rankin, Abednego Inman, Robert McFarland, Isaac Newman, Andrew Cowan, Isaac Barton, Tidence Lane, John Carson, Robert Elder, Nicholas Fain, Adam Meek,

112   Roy M. Rankin, Jefferson County Historical Society Newsletter, Vol. XIII, no. II, Spring 2001, 6.

George Turnley, James Roddye, and John Quarles. This list included the names of John Crockett and his brother William (David's father and uncle).

Early roads in the wilderness were the corridors along which communities and businesses were established. Through the 1790s, new settlers were arriving in ever-increasing numbers. An account in *A History of Tennessee and Tennesseans* states:

> In 1792-93, a road was laid out through the territory now included in Hamblen, and, extending to the western limits of Jefferson county, was met by the road from Knoxville. This road became a section of the stage route from Knoxville to Abingdon, Virginia. Settlers located along the road included William Chaney, Thomas Daggett [*sic* Doggett], Phelps Read, Richard Thompson, Isaac Martin, and John Crockett.[113]

A number of advertisements in early issues of the *Knoxville Gazette* made mention of roads in this part of eastern Tennessee, and documented the types of commerce occurring along the thoroughfares (such as postal delivery, leather tanning, iron works, and ferries). In 1792, John Chisolm published a notice that "Subscribers will establish a post [mail] from Knoxville to the Jefferson Courthouse (Dandridge), thence to Jonesboro, thence to Abingdon and return by Sullivan and Hawkins courthouses, to Knoxville, once every 21 days for 1 year."[114]

Adam Peck owned a mill on property where Mossy Creek empties into the Holston River, and advertised on May 4, 1793: "Ensuing season, commence the tanning and currying business at his plantation on

---

113   Will Thomas Hale and Dixon L. Merritt, *A History of Tennessee and Tennesseans*, Vol III (Lewis Publishing Co., 1913), 793.

114   The Dandridge Homecoming '86 Festival Committee, Edited and Compiled by Jean Bible, Jewell Hodge, Mary Jo Henry. *Historic Dandridge Yesterday and Today*, 1986, 8.

Mossy Creek, near Perkin's Iron Works. ... The road from Knoxville to Dodson's ford will in a short time be opened by the tan yard."

On Dec 29, 1793, Samuel Doak advertised: "The subscriber informs that he has a ferry established ... at his plantation on Holston, about six miles from Knoxville and four miles from the confluence of the French Broad and Holston. ... By this ferry it is the nearest way from Knoxville to Perkin's Iron works, Dumplin and Jefferson Courthouse."

Early maps are found in the University of Tennessee Library Special Collections, a number of which show some of the first roads going through old Jefferson County. One early map shows roads dating from 1795, titled "S.W. Territory," and showing a road that appears to follow the route of the Great Indian War Trail.[115] Another 1795 map titled "State of Tennessee" (which interestingly depicts Jefferson County *south* of Sevier County rather than the correct *north*) shows a single road running through "Jefferson" along the French Broad River, presumably meaning "Jefferson Courthouse" or the town of Dandridge.[116] Another map from 1796 titled "Tennessee: Lately the S.W.N: Territory" shows a road running south of Bays Mountain along the Nolichucky and French Broad Rivers.

Two maps from the Library of Congress, one from 1796[117] and a postal map from 1804[118] both show a single road running from Knoxville to Dandridge. The 1796 map shows the road from Dandridge continuing on to Greeneville, while the 1804 map continues the route from Dandridge to Cheek's Crossroads. Neither map shows a road

---

115   University of Tennessee Special Collections Library Map identified as "Scott, P45212," titled S.W. Territory 1795.

116   University of Tennessee Special Collections Library Map identified as #912.768, State of Tennessee, 1795.

117   Library of Congress, Div. of Maps, G3700, 1796, B7a. From a map in the British Museum 591307--523.40, 3rd Edition. Courtesy of Kathryn C. Cohn.

118   Abraham Bradley. Maps of the U. S. Exhibiting Post Roads....Post Offices, Stage Roads, Counties and Principal Mines. 5th Edition, 1804. Library of Congress, Div. of Maps, G3700, 1804.b, B7a. Courtesy of Kathryn C. Cohn.

to the north along the Holston River from Knoxville to Cheek's Crossroads, although one certainly did exist there by 1804.

Challenges for Early Jefferson County Settlers

For early settlers, the frontier could be an inhospitable and sparsely populated place. It was said that in 1786 when Adam Meek located on Beaver Creek in Quaker Valley, he had no White neighbors west of him, though Native Americans had long occupied the Indian Creek area south of the French Broad River. Several pioneer families had established homesteads in this area prior to 1790, disregarding treaties that prohibited settlement south of the French Broad River. Families who arrived in the area early included some of my relations, including the Lewis, Sehorn, Graham, Ponder, and Swann families. Other families who migrated into this area at an early date included the Cunningham, Turnley, Cowan, and Denton families. A fort or station operated from 1790 to 1795 at Strawberry Plains for protection against Indian attacks.

Hostilities with Native Americans were common in early Jefferson County and were on the increase in the early 1790s. Two members of the Lewis family, a twenty-one-year-old woman and an eight-year-old boy, were killed in an Indian attack near their home on Indian Creek. On the way to inter the Lewis family members in the Pine Chapel Graveyard, the burial party was again attacked. George Cunningham, a member of the burial party, was killed. He was buried along with the others.

As conflicts between Indian peoples and settlers would later subside, the Indian Creek neighborhood in Jefferson County would be visited by native Cherokees, returning in small numbers during the summers through the late 1800s. According to Jefferson County resident Nelle Rainwater Mills (born around 1896):

> Indians came over to fish and make baskets along the
> French Broad even when Daddy was a little boy and his

grandmother was living. They would stop and visit her and talk. They were also from Cherokee [North Carolina] where my grandparents came from, so Grandmother knew them and talked about their people.[119]

Danger on the frontier of early eastern Tennessee did not come only from conflict with Native Americans, however. Highwaymen and brigands who considered the frontier beyond the reach of the law regularly preyed on travelers. The 1796 journal of two traveling Moravians recounts that they "traveled on the highway that leads to Kentucky and Cumberland, we came today, a few miles beyond Col. Roddy's, to the place where the road divides, to the right in the direction of Kentucky and the left in the direction of Cumberland. Yesterday we had been warned against spending the night in this region, because many thievish vagabonds dwell there."[120]

In his *Narrative*, David Crockett recalled the dangers that go along with living among rough frontiersmen. He described the atmosphere at Abraham Wilson's Tavern near Panther Springs, where he worked for a time to pay off one of his father's debts. Crockett wrote:

> It was a place where a heap of bad company met to drink and gamble, and I wanted to get away from them, for I know'd very well if I staid there, I should get a bad name, as nobody could be respectable that would live there. [*N*, 45]

In *Sketches*, Matthew St. Clair Clarke noted: "The village [Panther Springs] had a bad character, and David protested against going." The Wilson Tavern was only a mile from the neighborhood of Quaker John Canaday on the headwaters of Panther Creek. Old Tavern, an inn run

119   Jean Patterson Bible, *Bent Twigs in Jefferson County* (Rogersville, TN: East Tennessee Printing Co., Inc., 1991), 47.

120   Samuel C. Williams, *Early Travels in the Tennessee Country* (Johnson City, TN: Wautaga Press, 1928), 452.

by John Evans, was on the old wagon road and was located between the Quakers and Abraham Wilson's place.[121]

The perceived dangers of the frontier even extended to the realm of superstition. For example, local lore and legend held that an area near Indian Creek, known as "The Diggins," which had been landscaped and terraced by Native people (likely for agriculture) was haunted. Local residents tended to avoid the area at night for fear of unfriendly spirits. While an 1836 district survey of Jefferson County referred to this area as "the dug hill,"[122] the earliest reference to this area appears on a 1797 Jefferson County deed, which called for the following tract in the area of the Diggins:

> ... on Indian Creek on the South side of the FBR ... up the old Waggon Road ... thence to a [road] known as the *dug* Road [part of the Diggins] thence to a lick above the burnt Cabin from thence to the old War Path ...[123]

Some of those new settlers included Adam Peck, who migrated with his wife, Elizabeth Sharkey Peck, from Botetourt County, Virginia, and began the first settlement at Mossy Creek (now Jefferson City) in 1788–89. Mentioned earlier, Adam Peck owned a mill on Mossy Creek, along with a leather tanning and currying business. A historical account noted that Peck had discovered on his property, beside a spring that flowed into a nearby creek, a small and abandoned blockhouse, which appeared quite old and had apparently been used by hunters or explorers prior to the Pecks' arrival in 1788. The abandoned blockhouse offered evidence that itinerant long hunters would take the time to fortify their outposts when deep in frontier territory.[124]

---

121   Maxine Mathews, *Old Inns of East Tennessee* (East Tennessee Historical Society Publications, 1928), 22–23.

122   1836 District Survey of Jefferson County, Tennessee.

123   Jefferson County Deed Book D, p. 218, Nov 29, 1797.

124   *Bicentennial Diamond Jubilee Celebration of Jefferson City*, 1901–1976, published

Colonel James Roddy, owner of a large farm called "Hayslope," was a prominent resident of Jefferson County. Roddy is buried in Bent Creek cemetery near his home (which was still standing in 2018). The old road from Charleston to Lexington passed through the Hayslope property (following the track of Daniel Boone when he traveled to "the dark and bloody ground" of Kentucky).

Other early property owners in the area included Elliott Grills, William Line (a close associate of David Crockett), Abraham Fitch, John Caldwell, and Quaker Joseph Reese[125] whose son Yarnell Reese married David Crockett's sister Betsy (for whom Crockett named his rifle). From a Quaker family, Yarnell Reese and wife, Betsy Crockett Reese, lived close by the rest of the Crockett family.[126] By 1797, between seventy-five and one hundred families had settled in the Mossy Creek neighborhood. Within a few short years, the population of the county went from no White settlers to a total of 7,840 people, according to a territorial census of 1795.

Political and Judicial Life

As the population of Jefferson County increased, so did the emergence of judicial systems to maintain social order. On March 21, 1792, William Blount, Governor of the Territory South of the River Ohio, ordained that a court be held in Jefferson and Knox Counties, to be known as the "Hamilton District." In Jefferson County, the courts were to be held on the north side of the French Broad River on the lands of Francis Dean (near the Reverend Mr. Henderson's Lower Meeting House, which is the present-day site of the town of Dandridge). On June 11, 1792, Jefferson and Knox Counties were formed out of parts

---

in 1976.

125   Goodspeed, *History of Tennessee* (Nashville: The Goodspeed Publishing Co., 1886).

126   Goodspeed, *History of Tennessee.*

of Greene and Hawkins Counties. The Jefferson County Court first met on July 22, 1792.[127]

By 1801, a group of Jefferson County residents filed a petition to the Tennessee State Legislature requesting that Grainger County be abolished and the land divided between Jefferson and Cocke Counties. Many of the petition's signatories had strong connections to the Crockett family, including Patterson Crockett (David's brother); John Canaday, Sr. (an old Quaker who was David Crockett's friend and longtime employer); Canaday's sons John Jr., Charles, Boater, and Robert (who married Amy Sumner, David's first love); William Bettis and Solomon Cox (Finley Gap residents with many connections to the Crockett family); Peter Cluck (David's landlord after his marriage to Polly Finley); and John Evans (tavern owner at Panther Springs).[128]

Commerce in Early Jefferson County

At the turn of the eighteenth century, few mercantile stores existed in sparsely inhabited areas like the one where David grew up in Jefferson County. Businesses tended to appear along thoroughfares like wagon roads, where they were most likely to encounter paying customers. Two of those early routes carried travelers out of the Virginia valley into eastern Tennessee and then onward to Kentucky. The northern route followed the Holston River (and became US Highway 11E, which passes through Rogersville, Russellville, and New Market to Knoxville). The southern route went through Bull's Gap and Dandridge to Knoxville.

Near Mossy Creek, Christopher Haynes took over the Perkins' Iron Works, which likely forged wagon rims and farm tools. The ironworks was located near the head of the creek and operated for a number of years.[129] Isaac Newman came to Mossy Creek in 1791 from

---

127   Ramsey, *Annals of Tennessee*, 576.

128   *Journal of Jefferson County Genealogical Society*, Dandridge, TN, April 2010, 33.

129   *Bicentennial Diamond Jubilee.*

North Carolina and was connected with the ironworks before turning to farming. Goodspeed's *History of Tennessee* noted that: "Thomas Humes, a professor at East Tennessee College in Knoxville, opened the first store in Mossy Creek prior to 1795 and was soon succeeded by Samuel Martin & Co."[130] The Hayworths, a Quaker family, were early farmers at the mouth of Mossy Creek.

Another of the early businesses established along Jefferson County thoroughfares was the Bent Creek Store, opened by Patrick Nenny sometime prior to 1796 near the main wagon road from Rogersville to Russellville (now US Highway 11E). The store was about eight miles from the site of John Crockett's Morristown tavern, on the southern route through a relatively remote area of today's Hamblen County. Nenny's employees included William Graham and his brother Hugh, who later married Nenny's daughter. Hugh Graham eventually became a partner in his father-in-law's store, that became known as Nenny & Graham.

Surviving records for the store's accounts are contained in the "Bent Creek Day Book," which serves as a useful historical reference. As the store was one of the few mercantile businesses in the area, its daybook provides a rich list of names of people who made purchases there, and who would have known the Crocketts personally. John Crockett was listed as a customer in the store's daybook on September 12 and 14, and October 4 and 30 of 1796, and on June 14 of 1797. The daybook lists a number of other customers who were served on those days, who would have likely rubbed shoulders with John Crockett. These other customers included Dicy Sturgeon, Abraham Fitch, Isaac Boorten, Major Robert McFarland, Vincent Lathim and William Lathim, Polly Brooks, William Donaldson, Capt. William White, Jonas Little, Gideon Morris, George Bean, William Russell, Micajah Lee, Wlisha Hurley, and William Beaver.

A list of other frequent customers included Charles Hodges, David and Hugh and John Kirkpatrick, John and Felty Houser, John Dodson,

---

130   Goodspeed, *History of Tennessee*, 862.

Thomas Kincaid, John Ryley, William Smith, George Evans, William and Jesse Cheek, and Jesse Green.

Other customers who frequented Nenny's Bent Creek Store and likely had Crockett connections included Caleb Witt, William Parks, Elizabeth Cheek, Tidence Lane, Edmond Hodges, Alexander Outlaw, Col. James Roddey, Aquilla Lane, William Moffet, Archibald Roane, Isaac Barton, James Shaddin, William Line, Dutton Lane, Joseph Hamilton, Ninian Chamberlain, Samuel Lane, Thomas Humes, George Bull, Samuel Wear, John Cox, and Daniel Inman.

Nenny's daybook provides some insight into John Crockett's specific purchases and transactions, and it provides documentation that John Crockett hired out at least two of his sons to work for Nenny in return for credit on payment toward tools and other supplies:

Patrick Nenny's Bent Creek Store
Bent Creek Daybook
May 1796–June 5, 1800

October 4, 1796—John Crockett bought "2 pegging awls; 1 cut knife; 2 ozs turkey yarn; 1.5 yards tarte."
> *Other persons in the store the same day: Richard Bird, Eliz Philpot, Annie MaHaffy, Alex W Do___, Timothy Holdaway & wife.*

October 30, 1796—John Crockett 1 Pint _____:
> *Other persons in the store the same day: John Lathim, Jerimiah Lathim, Daniel Anderson, Wm Mitchell, John Bull, Wm Smyth, Dira Sturgeon, David White.*

June 14, 1797—John Crockett "Credit for 7 weeks work of 2 sons last fall"
> *Other persons in the store the same day: Mrs. Harris, Geo Bean, Jas Mahon, Wm Rash, John Ester, Thomas Humes, Jerimiah Lathim, Negro Jack, Nathan White.*

John Crockett's Morristown Tavern

While John Crockett was a patron of area businesses like Nenny's Bent Creek Store, he also ran a business establishment of his own. John Crockett's tavern likely stood about seven or eight miles from the center of Morristown in the northeast quadrant. The success of a tavern like the one John Crockett was running depended heavily upon travelers who needed lodging—a crossroads would be an advantage in such an endeavor.

The present-day site of the Crockett Tavern Museum in Morristown is a reconstruction of the type of log cabin that would have housed an inn like the one established by John Crockett along the old wagon road. The reconstruction sits about one hundred yards north of the old wagon road (today US Highway 11E), and at a distance from the likely location of the original tavern, where a convenience store sits with gasoline tanks occupying the location of the tavern's cedar-lined well.[131]

Modern construction uncovered that cedar-lined well at the original site of Crockett's Tavern. On July 21, 1949, a Morristown newspaper headline announced: "WELL AT HOME OF DAVID CROCKETT, FAMED PIONEER, IS UNCOVERED HERE." The article noted that Herbert Smith was leveling off land with a bulldozer in connection with a woodworking plant being constructed by Harvey Stapleton in eastern Morristown:

> A. H. Dougherty [sic] of Russellville, authority on local history, stopped in 1945 when Mr. Stapleton was erecting his original plant, to tell him that David Crockett's well was located somewhere on the site Stapleton had purchased from J. D. Kreis. He walked over the land with the owner and marked almost the identical spot where broken earth was moved yesterday to reveal the still firm pieces of hand-hewn cedar that formed a three-foot box to line the well.

---

131   *Morristown Daily Gazette Mail*, July 21, 1949.

The article reported that Harvey Stapleton was making plans to preserve the site, which unfortunately never occurred. About seven years later on June 8, 1956, a deposition written by the same A. H. Daugherty of Morristown noted:

> Thomas Cain was a resident of Hamblen County and a Colonel in the Confederate Army. In about 1904 or 1905, he showed my father and me the site of the Crockett Tavern. We were standing at the spot. There was a slight sink on the surface of the ground. He said, "This is where the well was."
>
> A very slight elevation (now leveled off) just a little to the south-west of the well, same side of the railroad in where the tavern stood—only a few yards from the well. Col. Cain said that during the War Between the States, the old building was used as a pest house for smallpox. At the close of the war, about 90 years ago [which would have been about 1866], it was burned. A few years ago in grading for a warehouse, the well was uncovered just at the exact spot pointed out by Col. Cain. Some of the cedar boxing incasing the top of the well was intact. The railroad was built by this place over sixty years after the tavern was built.

It is unfortunate that the well could not have been preserved at the time it was rediscovered, with modern construction having destroyed any possibilities of further archeological research.

The Crockett legacy in Morristown is recognized in more than just the old tavern museum. Seven miles west of the tavern site, a geological feature is memorialized as "Crockett's Ridge"—a promontory with two peaks, one at about seventeen hundred feet and the taller one to the east at almost two thousand feet. The historical record is thin regarding exactly when the promontory became known as Crockett's Ridge.

According to one source, John Crockett moved onto land owned by James McGhee while he was building his tavern and readying it for use.[132] This area near Barton Spring would have been close to the present-day tavern site, and the area where David made his first formal attempts at schooling.

County records (confirmed by Goodspeed's *History of Tennessee*)[133] noted the names of property owners living in the vicinity of John Crockett and his tavern:

> About a mile east the Capps house was the home of Thomas Doggett, and continuing on, the home of Phelps Read. In the neighborhood were the residences of John Crockett, Richard Thompson, and Isaac Martin. Further to the east on the old Russellville Road, were homes of Isaac Barton, Joseph Shannon, and James McGhee.[134]

David and John Noes were two other local residents, living about three miles to the northwest of Crockett's Tavern. Those settlers frequenting Crockett's Morristown Tavern included those residing in the neighboring towns of Russellville and Whitesburg (east of Morristown along the old wagon road) and included the names of Samuel Riggs, James and William B. Roddye, William Pulliam, and Jesse Hoskins.

Also in the area was Caleb Witt, one of the earliest of the pioneer Baptist preachers, who along with Isaac Barton and Tidence Lane was credited with the formation of the Bent Creek Church near Whitesburg prior to 1794. This church became known as Bethel South of Holston, and later the First Baptist Church of Morristown.[135]

---

132   Jim Claborn, Hamblen County Historian.

133   Goodspeed, *History of Tennessee*, 868.

134   Hamblen County Centennial Committee, *Historic Hamblen, 1870–1970* (Morristown, TN, 1970), 29.

135   Goodspeed, *History of Tennessee*, 868.

Kitchen Schooling, Cheek's Crossroads, and a Cattle Drive

Young David Crockett first attended school in the fall of 1799. He recalled in his *Narrative* that the school: "… was kept in the neighborhood by a man whose name was Benjamin Kitchen; though I believe he was no way connected with the cabinet" [*N*, 29]. In his autobiography here, the adult David offered political sarcasm, making a tongue-in-cheek reference to his nemesis President Andrew Jackson and his group of unofficial advisors known as his "Kitchen Cabinet."

Benjamin Kitchen's school was located a short distance east of Barton's Spring near Russellville. On this site a few years later, the well-known Columbian Academy was founded."[136]

Benjamin Kitchen was listed as a customer in the daybook of the store at Cheek's Crossroads, located several miles from Crockett's Tavern and run by Jefferson County resident Jesse Cheek.[137] The Kitchens, Cheeks, and Crocketts were all certainly acquainted, with the store journal at Cheek's Crossroads also listing John and William Crockett as regular customers.[138]

As a resident of the area, Benjamin Kitchen was only a schoolteacher, but also linked to the community by marriage. Benjamin Catching [*sic*] married Elizabeth Caleb Witt on August 23, 1803, with a bond by her father, the Baptist preacher Caleb Witt (with the marriage record endorsed with the spelling of Benjamin "Kitching").[139] Caleb Witt received a grant (#1670) from the State of North Carolina in 1786, and settled near Russellville after the Revolutionary War.[140] A deed to Jesse Cheek at Cheek's Crossroads calls for land on "Fall

---

136 "The Crockett Tavern and Pioneer Museum" booklet.

137 Blomquist, A. K. *Cheek's Crossroads Tennessee, Store Journal 1802–1807* (Baltimore: Gateway Press, 2001), 117.

138 *Cheek's Crossroads Store Journal.*

139 Jefferson County Marriage Book I, p. 111.

140 Cora Davis Brooks, *History of Morristown 1787–1936* (Nashville, TN: Tennessee Historical Records Survey, Work Projects Administration, July 1940), 15.

Creek on waters of Holston river adjoining Caleb Witt."[141] Land deeds such as these provide supporting evidence that all were neighbors.

Though the families were clearly well acquainted, this was no guarantee that thirteen-year-old David's experience in Benjamin Kitchen's school would be without trouble. A 1955 Morristown newspaper story offered the following anecdote:

> By 1798, Benjamin Kitchen was teaching school on a hill nearby. One of these early settlers was John Crockett, who first located on what is known as the McGhee place near Barton Springs. By 1798, he had built a rough tavern a mile or two down the road. The exact location is known to be in East Morristown.
>
> David Crockett attended the school of Benjamin Kitchen for four days, then he ran away from home. Stopping at Barton's that morning, he announced that he was leaving. Isaac Barton begged him to return to his father's home, but he said he would run away rather than go back to "Old Kitchen's school."

Apparently, David had been involved in a fight after school with one of the other "scholars," as he called his schoolmates. David was afraid to return to school, and for the next several days pretended to go—until his father got wind of it. David pleaded with his father not to make him return to the school of old Kitchen, lest he "… be cooked up to a cracklin, in little or no time." David recounted that his father "… would whip me an eternal sight worse …" if he did not go on back to school [N, 31].

"My father had been taking a few horns [of liquor], and was in a good condition to make the fur fly," David continued. "Finding me rather too slow about starting, he gathered about a two-year-old

---

141   Jefferson County Deeds, Vol C, p. 317.

hickory, and broke after me." David ran about a mile with his father in hot pursuit, escaping his father's wrath by topping a hill and hiding on the far side until his father passed "puffing and blowing" then waiting "until he gave up the hunt and passed back again" [N, 32].

David was worried about having to face both his father and the schoolmaster Kitchen (whom he said, if they had both gotten ahold of him, they would have "used me up").

David recounted that he "… then cut out and went to the house of an acquaintance a few miles off, who was just about to start with a [cattle] drove. The acquaintance's name was Jesse Cheek, and I hired myself to go with him." David's "… elder brother, who also hired on to go" was already there [N, 32].

Conflict arose between the Crockett and Cheek families over young David embarking on this cattle drive to Virginia and Washington with Jesse Cheek (described in more detail in the following chapter). In *Sketches* [33], Matthew St. Clair Clarke stated that John Crockett had initiated a prosecution "… against the cattle driver who had carried him [David] off." Though David indicated that he went along with the Cheeks of his own free will, John Crockett's legal action over losing the services of his son resulted in him eventually receiving restitution, which illustrates how even thirteen-year-old children of the time were considered a valuable asset and labor resource. John Crockett seemed to always be living by a thread, and the need for even a child's potential earnings put pressure on the whole family to contribute.

David's problems with his schoolmaster are reminiscent of a story Daniel Boone liked to tell. Boone recalls "his teacher was an Irishman who would sneak out into the woods where he kept a hidden bottle of liquor." Boone located the teacher's liquor bottle and added a "purging potion" [laxative] to it. Boone found the outcome too funny to conceal, which resulted in his identifying himself as the perpetrator of the prank. When the teacher tried to use the rod on Daniel, Daniel knocked the teacher to the floor and went home. But, unlike in David Crockett's experience, Boone's mother, upon hearing of it, did not make him return to the Irishman's school. This type of story seems to reflect "boilerplate American folklore."[142] Folklore though it may be, Crockett's story was authentic and happened just as David reported: running from his father and ending up in long exile on a Virginia cattle drive.

David in the Home of Reverend Isaac Barton

The obligation of a young boy to work and contribute earnings to the family coffers was not limited to cattle drives. For a time, David also worked for Reverend Isaac Barton (1745–1831) and even lived in a second-floor room of Reverend Barton's log house.[143] Barton's home was on the old Holston Road in Morristown, less than two miles from the Crockett Tavern site, in an area known as Barton's Spring. With his wife, Keziah, Isaac Barton came to Greeneville, Tennessee, in 1780, and established himself at Warrensburg Church. Barton moved to Bent Creek Church and became associated with Reverend Tidence Lane at Whitesburg Church, where he remained for thirty-one years. A parting of the ways with Reverend Lane resulted in the creation of the Bethel South of Holston Church in 1800.[144]

In the Bethel Church minutes of Saturday, February 4, 1803, Reverend Barton documented a baptismal ceremony, along with those in attendance:

Met at Samuel Riggs and received by baptism Thomas. Majors Lemuel Hibain [*sic*] Gideon Tomson, Lydda Roddy, Rebecca Austin, *Rebecca Crocit,* Elizabeth Tomson, Mary Clowers, Rhoda Currey.[145]

---

142 John Mack Faragher, *Daniel Boone The Life and Legend of an American Pioneer* (New York: Henry Holt & Co., 1992), 15–16.

143 Don Floyd, *Morristown Citizen Tribune*, June 23, 1968, page 5. Obtained from Mrs. Foy Quarles.

144 J. J. Burnett, *Sketches of Tennessee's Pioneer Baptist Preachers* (Nashville: Marshall & Bruce, 1919), 38.

145 Bethel South of Holston Baptist church minutes roll book. Nolichucky Baptist Assoc. archives on Morris Blvd. in Morristown, TN.

Given the time and location, it is likely that this "Rebecca Crocit" was David's mother.

Barton's original house, built about 1800, is still standing, thanks to generations of owners who value historic preservation. The original part of Barton's home is much the same as in Crockett's day. In fact, the second-floor room once occupied by the young frontiersman, looking much as it did when the boy slept there, is still known as "Davy Crockett's Room."[146] The house and grounds, which include a large spring flowing from beneath a massive rock shelf, maintains a character and sense of antiquity equaled by few remaining structures. The Isaac Barton home is listed on the National Register of Historic Places.

John Crockett's Debts

Much has been made of John Crockett's unpaid debts, and the obligations he put on his children to provide earnings to the family purse. It is worth considering that the economic system of the time was based on a modified barter system, with debts being paid by traded goods or services, and coin or currency not serving as the primary instruments of payment. Credit extended to community members was common as a means of commerce. Just as the pace of life was slower, so, often, was the interval of repayment. Evaluations of the "creditworthiness" or financial stability of frontier families struggling to subsist should be assessed within the cultural context of the time.

Nevertheless, John Crockett apparently had his share of problems with indebtedness. He owed Gideon Morriss for 35 bushels of Indian corn from 1783 until Morriss's death in 1798—and that debt was likely never repaid. A revealing one-word comment appears in the accounts

---

146   Margo Helms, "Barton Springs; Davy Crockett Slept Here," *Morristown Daily Gazette,* November 13, 1966.

of Morriss's estate list, noting what would appear to be the condition of the debtor as "Desperate."[147]

It looks as if John Crockett's financial prospects had not improved three years later when, in July 1801, he was sued by Jesse Riggs in Grainger County.[148] Crockett likely had an unpaid debt to Riggs, who operated a "still house" just across the Grainger County line near Morristown.

Regarding ownership and indebtedness on the property where John Crockett's Tavern sat, there is historical evidence that the property owner—and thus John Crockett's landlord on the Morristown tavern—was John Canaday. (See Appendix D: Chain of Land Ownership—Crockett's Tavern Site.) This would explain why Canaday had a credit note against Crockett, which David agreed to work off for his father. In his *Narrative,* David wrote:

> I was certain enough that I should never get any part of the note [the one he had worked off to Quaker John Canaday at Panther Springs] but then I remembered it was my father that owed it, and I concluded it was my duty as a child to help him along, and ease his lot as much as I could. I told the Quaker I would take him up at his offer, and immediately went to work. I never visited my father's house during the whole time of this engagement, though he lived only fifteen miles off.[149]

John was not the only member of the Crockett family to have troubles repaying his debts. On October 17, 1808, a William Crockett (probably David's brother and not his uncle) was listed as having an outstanding debt against the estate of Miller Doggett (probably a brother of Jesse Doggett and uncle of Thomas Doggett, who would

---

147 Jefferson Co. Will Book #1, p. 176, May 9, 1798.

148 Grainger County Order Book, p. 30.

149 *Narrative,* 46.

later serve as bondsman for David on his license to marry Polly Finley). Also listed as creditors of the estate are Isaac Barton and Abraham Wilson, both connected with John and David Crockett.[150] On October 10, 1820, a William Crockett, presumably the same man, sold an enslaved person to Charles Hodges, a known resident of the Morristown neighborhood.[151]

David and His Parents in Jefferson County

While David mentions his father, John, frequently in his *Narrative*, his autobiography rarely mentions his mother, Rebecca, at all. In her conspicuous absence from his memoir, it may be that she had little influence on his early life, or that she had an influence, and for whatever reason, he chose not to share his thoughts about her.

The picture he paints of his father, on the other hand, is more detailed—and depicts a man having a hard time grinding out a living, with little luck on his side. John will indenture his son at age twelve to a stranger traveling hundreds of miles, without making any arrangements for his return. John drinks prodigious amounts of liquor and tries to beat David with a stout rod, prompting David's departure from home for some two-and-a-half years. On the other hand, John does attempt to provide his children with education. David recounts his father's tears of appreciation when David surprises him with the paid-off note owed to Quaker John Canaday.

It is clear, however, that one must reserve the impulse to judge the pioneers of the 1790s by social standards we embrace in the twenty-first century. John Crockett's behavior as a father during their time in Jefferson County, at least in David's eyes as reflected in his *Narrative*, does not seem to deviate far from the norm of the times. David reflected on his home and family in a touching way and

---

150   Oct. 17, 1808, William Crockett debt against the estate of Miller Doggett. Jefferson County records.

151   Jefferson County Court Book 1, p. 128.

described his homesickness while indentured to Jacob Siler [N, 24], an experience we'll explore in the following chapter.

Of his Jefferson County years, David seemed to accept that life on the frontier is hard and a person should demonstrate the strength to make the best of it.

CHAPTER 9:

Bound for Virginia and Back

Young David Crockett's sixteen years living in Jefferson County were punctuated by two separate excursions to Virginia. The first occurred in 1798 when John Crockett hired out twelve-year-old David to a passing stockman, Jacob Siler of Rockbridge County, Virginia. Siler, then age thirty-five, had come west from Virginia to Tennessee to acquire a herd of cattle, which he was driving back east to his father-in-law's property in Virginia. On his cattle drive, Siler stopped at the Crockett tavern in Morristown and arranged that David be bound over to him to assist on the cattle drive.

Involuntary Indentured: 1798

In his *Narrative*, David recounted:

> An old Dutchman by name of Jacob Siler, who was moving from Knox county to Rockbridge, in the state of Virginia, in passing, made a stop at my father's house. He had a large stock of cattle that he was carrying with him; and I suppose made some proposition to my father hire some one to assist him.

> … as young as I was, and as little as I knew about traveling,

or being away from home, he hired me to the old Dutchman, to go the four hundred miles on foot, with a perfect stranger that I had never seen until the evening before. I set out with a heavy heart, it is true, but I went ahead until we arrived at a place, which was three miles from what is called Natural Bridge, and made a stop at the house of Mr. Hartley, who was father-in-law to Mr. Siler, who had hired me. My Dutch master was very kind to me, and gave me five or six dollars, being pleased, as he said, with my services. [*N*, 22]

The route of Siler's cattle drive, with young David assisting, would likely have followed the path marked by present-day Interstate 81, which passes within five miles of the drive's origin in Morristown and its destination in Virginia. While Crockett's *Narrative* recounts that his odyssey covered a distance of four hundred miles, he was likely including the distance of a return trip, as the distance from his father's tavern in Morristown to Natural Bridge in Virginia is about 240 miles.

It was not uncommon at the time for poor frontier families to indenture or hire out their sons once the lads reached adolescence. The practice served to reduce the number of mouths to feed in a household and could also help the *pater familias* reduce his outstanding debts.[152] There is documentation of John Crockett making use of his son's labor to help pay for supplies and provide for the family's household. An earlier accounting in Patrick Nenny's "Bent Creek Daybook" indicated that John received credit at the store for seven weeks of work performed by two of the older Crockett sons in the fall of 1796.[153] Nevertheless, John Crockett's indenturing of a son as young as twelve to a stranger who would take him hundreds of miles from his home—apparently with no arrangements for his return—spoke to the financial straits the elder Crockett must have found himself in.

---

152   Mark Derr, *The Frontiersman: The Real Life and Many Legends of David Crockett* (New York: William Morrow Press, 1995).

153   June 14, 1797, Bent Creek Daybook, May 1796–June 5, 1800.

Who Was Jacob Siler?

Although Crockett's *Narrative* referred to Jacob Siler as "a Dutchman," the name of Siler (with spelling variations including Sëyler, Seiler, Sylar, Saylor, and others) is in fact a Germanic name, which translates to "rope maker." While his autobiography referred to Siler as "an old Dutchman," Siler family history states that Jacob (born in 1763 in Frederick County, Maryland), was son to Johann Jacob Sëyler, who was born in 1749 in the Alsace-Lorraine region that borders France and Germany. This would make Jacob Siler more German than Dutch.[154]

As to David's description of thirty-five-year-old Jacob Siler as "old," it is certainly understandable that a twelve-year-old would consider any adult over the age of thirty as being ancient.

Although Jacob Siler was, at the time of this cattle drive, a resident of Virginia, he and his father-in-law were acquiring land in Tennessee. Property records from Knox County show a deed from Peter Hardley ([*sic*] Hartley) to Jacob Syler ([*sic*] Siler), dated March 18, 1799. This deed recorded a payment of $33.33 for 150 acres on the south side of the Holston River, being a part of a tract originally granted to William Davidson, and bounded by Joseph Jackson's and James Jackson's property lines. The deed was witnessed by Joseph and Robert Evans.[155] Another Knox County deed to Jacob Siler from John Brown for 199 acres on Lyons Creek in Knox County was dated May 20, 1808.[156] The property lay on both sides of Lyons Creek, originally a part of a tract granted to William Brown on December 20, 1791, joining lands of David W. Nowell and Felex Brown. This deed was witnessed by Joseph Evans, John Rensbargar, and Alexander McMillin.

A Jacob Siler is mentioned in the book *Foxfire 5* as an ancestor of C. E. (Bud) Siler of Asheville, North Carolina (himself a maker of fine Kentucky rifle locks). The *Foxfire 5* book states that "Jacob Siler was supposed to have made a gun for Daniel Boone. The rifle has been in

---

154   The Siler Family. http://www.sonsofdewittcolony.org/mckstorysylar1.htm.

155   Knox County Deed Book E-2, p. 92.

156   Knox County Deed Book N, Vol 1, p. 122.

a private home near Washington, DC. That ancestor was supposed to have moved south from Pennsylvania with the Boone family."[157] The town of Springfield is mentioned with regard to the Silers and the Hartleys, and that town is located near Natural Bridge, Virginia.

In personal correspondence with this author, Bud Siler says of his ancestor: "I have an idea that the Jacob Siler [who] Davy tells about may very well be the Siler I refer to in *Foxfire 5*, though I can't document it. He did live at Natural Bridge, Virginia. His ancestor came from Germany in 1741 to Pennsylvania and by 1753 was living on John's Creek in southwest Virginia. By 1764, he moved to North Carolina. Siler City was named for him. Jacob Siler is mentioned in *Kegley's Virginia Frontier* along with a Peter Hartley, who almost certainly is the Hartley that Davy mentions.[158] It also refers to the town of Springfield near Natural Bridge and lists the earliest settlers that includes Jacob "Cyler" and Peter Hartley. It says "the 'Silors' were gunmakers who knew the Boones in Pennsylvania."[159]

If indeed this is the same Jacob Siler who took young David Crockett into his employ as a twelve-year-old cattle drover and who also made a rifle for Daniel Boone, Siler would be one of the few physical connections between the two American frontier icons—Crockett and Boone—who were born more than fifty years apart and otherwise never met or corresponded. Any rifle made by Jacob Siler would be of special interest, considering the background of its maker.

Jacob Siler is noted in his family history as having moved from Virginia to "Knox and/or Roane County, Tennessee," around 1807 or 1808. An obituary appeared in the *Knoxville Register*, noting Jacob Siler's passing on 16 March 1826 in Roane County, Tennessee.[160]

---

157   Eliot Wigginton, *Foxfire 5* (Garden City, NY: Anchor Press/Doubleday, 1979), 283.

158   Frederick Bittle Kegley, *Kegley's Virginia Frontier* (Genealogical Publishing Co., 1938), 435.

159   C. E. (Bud) Siler, Asheville, North Carolina. Letter dated September 10, 1990.

160   The Siler Family. http://www.sonsofdewittcolony.org/mckstorysylar1.htm.

Escape from Virginia

Returning to the story of David's servitude under Jacob Siler in 1798, after a foot journey of about 240 miles, David indicated in his *Narrative* that "… we arrived at the place, which was three miles from what is called the Natural Bridge, and made a stop at the house of a Mr. Hartley, who was father-in-law to Mr. Siler." David wrote that Siler treated him "very kindly," but that he thought it "was bait for me, as he persuaded me to stay with him and not return any more to my father. I had been taught so many lessons of obedience by my father, that I at first supposed I was bound to obey this man, or at least I was afraid to openly disobey him; and I therefore staid [*sic*] with him, and tried to put on a look of contentment until I got the [Siler-Hartley] family all to believe I was fully satisfied." [*N*, 23]

After four or five weeks of working for Siler and Hartley, David was playing along a roadside when he happened upon three passing wagons, one driven by a man named Dunn. David knew the man from his frequent stops at his father's tavern in Morristown. Dunn told David that he was carrying a load of goods to Knoxville. David told Mr. Dunn that he wanted to return home, and Dunn agreed to bring him along, and to protect him if they were pursued.[161] David laid plans to sneak out of the Hartley house that night and join Dunn the next morning at a tavern seven miles away, with the instructions that he must arrive before the wagons left at dawn.

When David crept out of the Hartley house three hours before daylight, snow was falling fast. Eight inches lay on the ground and there was no moon. "I had to guess at my way to the big road … I could not have pursued the big road if I had not guided myself by the opening it made between the timber. … Before I overtook the waggons, the earth was covered about as deep as my knees" [*N*, 25]. He was careful to avoid being apprehended, lest he be returned to his involuntary service with the Silers and Hartleys. He knew if this happened, "he would have little chance of escape … though I was a wild boy, yet I dearly

---

161   Narrative pg. 22-23

loved my father and mother, and their images appeared to be so deeply fixed in my mind" [N, 24].

David arrived at the tavern with an hour to spare before daylight. Over two hours, David had traveled seven miles in ever-deepening snow in the pitch dark. This would be quite an accomplishment even for a grown man, and a remarkable feat for a boy of just twelve years.

After a while on the road, David decided to part company with Dunn's slow-moving wagons, thinking he could make better time on his own. Along that same road, David later met a man "returning from market, to which he had been with a drove of horses," somewhere near the first crossing of the Roanoke River. David wrote in his *Narrative*: "He had a led a horse, with a bridle and saddle on him, and he kindly offered to let me get on his horse and ride him." David traveled with this man "until we got within 15 miles of my father's house. There we parted, and he went on to Kentucky [likely at Cheek's Crossroads] and I trudged on homeward" [N, 26].

Survival on the frontier often came down to self-reliance, native intelligence, energy, and force of will—qualities David demonstrated even at this early age. Although self-reliance is key, gaining allies and obtaining help from others is critical to surviving in the wilderness. Twelve-year-old David demonstrated these abilities aptly. Clearly, his desire to return to his family provided him the motivation and inspiration to overcome mental and physical adversity. In addition, he demonstrated the fortitude and wherewithal to plan and execute his escape from the Hartley house, even when confronted with an unexpected snow that made an arduous task all the more difficult. A person who survives such tests emerges stronger, smarter, and more confident. Twelve-year-old David rose to the challenges of extricating himself from a situation of near-captivity and finding his way home.

The author is indebted to the late Mrs. Katheryn Cohn of McLean, Virginia, a dedicated Crockett researcher, who helped document David's odyssey back to Tennessee. Using an 1804 map found in the Library of Congress, she was able to help show David's likely route from Abingdon, Virginia, through Blountville and Rogersville and back to Morristown.

A Virginia Cattle Drive and Other Occupations: Fall 1799 to Spring 1802

Only recently having repatriated himself to Tennessee from Virginia after being involuntarily indentured to Jacob Siler, his next cattle-driving adventure east was wholly voluntary. His first excursion east to Virginia lasted a couple of months. This time, David stayed gone for two-and-a-half years.

The Cheek's cattle drive ran from Abingdon to Lynchburg, by the Orange County Courthouse, and from there, on to Charlottesville and through Chester Gap to Front Royal, where Cheek sold his cattle to a man named Vanmetre. Interestingly, a John Vanmeter had been a pioneer and large landowner near Front Royal when Davy's grandfather David had lived in the area from 1743–1770.

After Cheek's cattle were delivered, David started back home with a brother of Jesse Cheek. With only one horse between them, the elder Cheek was inhospitable in sharing the saddle. When David had enough of being the only one walking, he told Cheek to go on alone and he would get himself home.

While on the road, David met a man named Adam Myers, a wagoner from Greeneville, Tennessee, who was traveling north to Gerrardstown (in present-day West Virginia). Myers was traveling north—the opposite direction David was headed. However, David decided he was in no hurry to see his father because "his anger would hang on to him like a turkle [turtle] does to a fisherman's toe" [N, 33]. So David joined Myers and postponed the eventual confrontation his returning home would inevitably cause. On the road heading east, David met his elder brother with whom he'd started on Cheek's cattle drive. His brother tried but could not persuade David to return home with him.

At one point, David parted ways with Adam Myers and began working in Gerrardstown for a farmer named John Gray. His wage was twenty-five cents a day. John Gray's farm was very near the farm once owned by David's grandfather, where his father John grew up (in Nollville, just west of Martinsburg, West Virginia). David's *Narrative* makes no mention of his being aware of this fact. He worked on John Gray's farm for several months. In the spring of 1800, he used some of his hard-earned money to buy a new set of clothes. This would have been no small investment for a boy like David, with the manufacturing of clothing involving a laborious process and commanding a hefty price.

Crockett later rejoined Adam Myers and took on work hauling barrels of flour from Gerrardstown to Baltimore. David must have trusted Myers, as he gave Myers seven dollars of his own money to hold for safekeeping. On the way to Baltimore, David was in the back of the wagon near Ellicott's Mill when some of the flour barrels broke loose, which caused the horses to spook and bolt. A rough ride ensued, ending at a sharp turn when the wagon tongue broke simultaneously with both axletrees. David recalled in his *Narrative*: "Even a rat would have stood a bad chance in a straight race among them [the barrels], and not much better in a crooked one. ... But this proved to me, that if a fellow is born to be hung, he will never be drowned" [*N*, 35–36]. David's sardonic wit showed through and proved his destiny was not to suffer so obscure an ending as being crushed by a rogue flour barrel.

Nearly a Merchant Sailor

Upon arriving in Baltimore with their load of flour, David went to the wharf. There he met a ship's captain who invited him to join his merchant crew on a voyage to London. David agreed and went to retrieve his new clothes and his seven dollars from Adam Myers, who steadfastly refused to relinquish either. Myers presumed to confine David within his sight until they turned homeward. David recounted that Myers was cross with him and even threatened him with the whip. Although David didn't consider it at the time, Myers may have foreseen the potential for danger at sea, especially on a ship that would take him so far away from home. David's *Narrative* doesn't reflect any introspection on his lack of maritime knowledge, nor of the potential difficulties in returning home from such a sea voyage. Had it not been for Myers stopping him, David's life would have turned out quite differently.

Regardless, David ran away from Myers that night, leaving without his seven dollars (the equivalent of about $150 today). He traveled a short distance down the road, where he encountered another wagoner, also named Myers: Henry Myers from Pennsylvania. In David's loneliness and unhappiness of what seemed like a hopeless situation, he sought out the man's help. David broke into tears as he told this man of the treatment he had received from Adam Myers, who was still in possession of David's little bit of money.

David recalled that Henry Myers was "a very large, stout looking man, and as resolute as a tiger," and that he "became exceedingly angry" to hear of David predicament [*N*, 38]. Henry Myers took David back two miles to confront the other wagoner and demanded he hand over the boy's money. Henry Myers chastised Adam Myers, admonishing him: "You damn'd rascal, you have treated this boy badly." Adam Myers replied that it was David's fault, and he claimed to have already spent David's money. The confrontation ended, and Henry Myers later took up a collection for David at their next stop where other wagon-drivers were assembled. From among them, they gave David three dollars to begin his long journey home.

Records from Greene County, Virginia, contain the will of one Adam Myers, written December 7, 1816, and filed January 25, 1824. This document lists a wife, Mary, sons John and William, and daughters Phebe Roberts and Polly Bullard. The executors are Alexander Armstrong and John Rogers and witnessed by Nathaniel Smith and Christopher Miller. The will is signed with an X as "his mark."[162] It is

---

162   Greene County Will Book, Adam Myers, registered 25 Jan. 1824, written 7 Dec 1816.

likely that this is the same Adam Myers for whom David worked in Virginia.

A Year and a Half in Christiansburg

The three dollars donated by the charitable wagon masters took David as far as Montgomery Courthouse at Christiansburg, Virginia, where he settled in and lived for more than a year and a half. The town of Christiansburg was named for Revolutionary War soldier William Christian, who had led a group of soldiers into the Tennessee country against the Cherokees, who were at that time allied with the British. Colonel Christian's 1777 march took him right through what would later become David's home grounds in eastern Tennessee. John Crockett, David's father, may have been on one of those expeditions. Many of the men on that march became the first settlers of East Tennessee when they returned there to claim land and settle, captivated by the beauty of the region they'd first seen while on campaign. David secured a job on the farm of James Caldwell of Montgomery County, where he worked one month and was paid five dollars.

Elijah Griffith and a Hat-Making Apprenticeship

At the end of his job with farmer Caldwell, David bound himself to a hatter named Elijah Griffith, who lived and operated his business in Christiansburg. David was to work as Griffith's apprentice for a period of four years, a typical length of time for an apprenticeship. However, David had worked at this job for only a year and a half when Griffith became so far in debt that he "left the country." For all his eighteen months of labor at this hat-making apprenticeship, David had received no pay, and no more than his room and board [N, 40].

One has to wonder why David stayed that long for only room and board, although it ended up being to David's benefit, again, that he did not work for Griffith any longer than he did. At this time, hatters worked with lead in the process of making hats—and many of them died young from lead poisoning.

The 1810 census of Virginia (about a decade after David's apprenticeship) listed one Elijah Griffith residing in Fauquier County, Virginia, about two hundred miles northeast of Montgomery County.[163]

By now in the spring of 1802, David decided to make use of the hat-making skills he had gained under Griffith before the man abandoned his business. In a history of Montgomery County, Lula Givens wrote about David's stay in Christiansburg, saying, "Davy Crockett lived in Christiansburg for a time and worked at John Snider's Hattery Shop. He stayed on, and in Snider's Hattery Shop he worked at the hatter's trade. John Snider's residence was where Legget's Store is now [historical account published 1981]. The Hattery Shop was where the Barber shop and Dixon's Jewelry Shop are."[164] David's *Narrative* does not give much information concerning Elijah Griffith, Snider's hattery shop, or much at all of his time in Montgomery County. It may be worth noting that a John Griffith of Montgomery County, Virginia, had bought in 1787, "188 acres on the South Fork of the Holston being the lower end of the Joseph Crockett *Patton* [patent]."[165]

David's account of his stay in Montgomery County is brief, considering that he stayed there for a year and a half. It may be that he chose not to reflect on the bad experiences he had there, with men who had taken advantage of his labor and then failed to pay him. A branch of the Crockett family has had a long history in Montgomery County, however. A number of Crocketts were living in Montgomery at the time David was there. A John Crockett had sold, on March 7, 1780, two hundred acres of land in Montgomery County, Virginia.[166] There is a Crockett's Creek in Montgomery County and Crocketts with the

---

163   Elizabeth P. Bentley, *Index to the 1810 Census of Virginia* (Baltimore: Genealogical Publishing Co., 1980).

164   Givens, *Christiansburg, Montgomery County, Virginia* 37.

165   Montgomery County Virginia, Deed Book A, 1773–1789, p. 489.

166   Kegley, *Kegley's Virginia Frontier.*

names of Jean, Alexander, Andrew, Anthony, David, Elisabeth, Esther, Hugh, Jacob, Jane, James, John, Joseph, Margaret, Robert, Samuel, Walter, and William are all listed as having resided there between 1769 and 1800.[167]

In a 1782 listing of taxpayers of Montgomery County, there appears the name of William Finley (the name of David's future father-in-law) and a John Crockett, David's father's name. Both are listed again in August of 1789.[168] A March 1784 deed in adjacent Botetourt County lists a Joseph Hawkins (the name of David's uncle).[169]

David says in his *Narrative* that his reason for staying in Christiansburg so long was that his three-dollar donation from the generous wagon-drivers ran out at that place in his journey. It's also possible that David decided to stay in Christiansburg because he had relatives there, or knew people there who were in some way connected with his family.

Obviously, David was in no hurry to get home, but it remains curious why David chose to stay in Christiansburg for eighteen months and why he would not have commented on the odd circumstance of finding himself in a place surrounded by so many people with his own surname. He fails to mention any family connections to the numerous Crocketts who lived around him in Montgomery County. It seems likely there is more to this story than David reveals or takes time to tell. He glosses over a significant span of time in telling his story at this place and leaves it to speculation why he tarried so long. He indicates that he set about working at odd jobs to get enough money to buy clothes to make his trip back home.

The most significant thing that happened to David in Montgomery County involved his decision on when and how to leave. After his eighteen-month stay in Christiansburg, David was finally ready to

---

167   L. P. Summers, *Annals of Southwestern Virginia 1769–1800* (Abingdon, Virginia, 1929).

168   Summers, *Annals of Southwestern Virginia 1769–1800.*

169   Botetourt County, Virginia, Deed Book #3, p. 226.

continue his long journey home. He departed Christiansburg, walking in a southwesterly direction for about ten miles (likely following the approximate route of today's Interstate 81, going southwest out of Christiansburg, then reaching the New River where the Little River joins it). The point David was seeking was where the Wilderness Road crossed the New River, about a mile downstream from the mouth of the Little River.

David found at this point a ferry station, where in 1762, William Ingles was given license to operate a ferry across the New River. In 1773, Ingles began operating a public house in addition to his ferry service. "Ingles Ferry and Tavern" is today a Virginia Historic Landmark and is on the National Register of Historic Places.

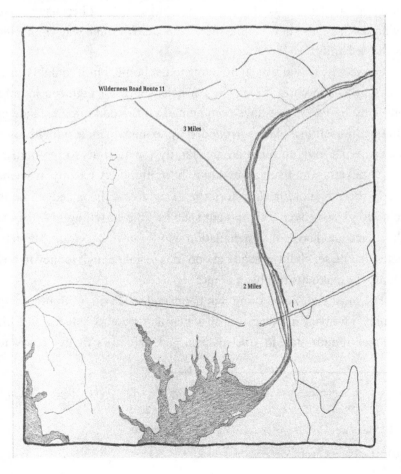

David indicates that he started walking upstream, perhaps looking for a canoe after ferry operators refused to operate in the cold and stormy weather. Given the context of David's statement, it would seem likely he was at the mouth of the Little River when he began his crossing. Although strongly counseled not to attempt it, David did manage to borrow a canoe and set out to cross the treacherous water: "I found it a mighty ticklish business, I tell you. … I turned the canoe across the waves, to do which, I had to turn it nearly up the river, as the wind came from that way; and I went about two miles before I could land" [*N*, 41]. When he did land the canoe, it was half-filled with water and his clothes were frozen on him. Desperate to get warm, David traveled three bone-chilling miles before coming to a house where he could warm and dry himself by a fire [*N*, 41].

From there he proceeded to Sullivan County, Tennessee, where he stayed for a while with his brother who had originally traveled with him to Front Royal. It is likely that this brother was Aaron Crockett, an older brother who was known to have lived in Sullivan County.[170] David lingered in Sullivan County, indicating that he was still in no hurry to get back to his father's tavern even after so long a time away. After two-and-a-half years away from home, he still appeared to be afraid to face his father.

The reader is often reminded in the *Narrative* of the incredible hardships and dangers of life and travel during this early time and the toughness necessary to survive. David's account demonstrates his determination to pursue his objectives and even, at times, taking unnecessary risks. During his two-and-a-half years on his own as a young teenager, David Crockett was nearly lost to the sea, crushed by a flour barrel, had his money and clothes stolen, been lead-poisoned, and nearly drowned in a river. Yet he endured.

---

170 Kathryn Coe Cohn, Letter, August 5, 1992—"I have firm proof of Crockett Brothers William, Patterson, John and very likely Aaron of Sullivan County …"

David Arrives Back Home

David recounted that he arrived at home and mixed in for the evening meal with other travelers assembled at his father's tavern. He remained slyly anonymous, until one of his sisters finally recognized him—to much excitement.

"The joy of my sisters and my mother, and, indeed, all of the family, was such that it humbled me, and made me sorry that I hadn't submitted to a hundred whippings, sooner than cause so much affliction as they had suffered on my account." David indicated that "the joy of my father, occasioned by my unexpected return, I was sure would secure me against my long-dreaded whipping; and so, they did" [*N*, 43].

A similar story of youthful solo adventure appears in the life of Daniel Boone (whom Crockett never met). Boone related that he had returned home to the upper Yadkin River in northwestern North Carolina in May 1771 after an extended period of captivity among the Indians. There was a neighborhood frolic in progress and no one recognized him in his beard and dirty clothes. Boone saw his wife, Rebecca, standing by and watching the dancing. He walked over to her and asked her to dance, an offer she quickly declined. He said laughing, "You need not refuse, you have danced with me many times." Recognizing him, Rebecca threw her arms around him weeping as the amazed neighbors looked on in disbelief at "Mrs. Boone's inappropriate behavior with some old wayfaring hunter."[171]

When David left his home in East Tennessee, he had been barely thirteen years old. Now he had spent two-and-a-half years completely on his own. He had been exposed to many challenges. He had seen large cities and worked at a variety of jobs. His experiences with both employers and with strangers had taught him important life lessons. He left his home a novice in the ways of the world but returned a person who understood considerably more about himself—what he wanted and what he valued. He had faced many challenges on his own and had survived. Those lessons gave him a maturity that helped

---

171   Faragher, *Daniel Boone The Life and Legend*, 87.

him make sound, important choices in the next chapter of his life. Against great odds, David Crockett was beginning to rise above his circumstances.

CHAPTER 10:

Rough Taverns and Staid Quakers at Panther Springs

After his eastern adventures as a cattle drover, hat maker, and nearly as an enlisted seaman, the almost seventeen-year-old David related that in the spring of 1802, his father had asked him for help. It seemed that John Crockett had gotten himself indebted to fellow tavern owner Abraham Wilson in the amount of thirty-six dollars (the equivalent of about nine hundred dollars today). John asked the boy to help his poor old dad by working off the debt, and David agreed. The arrangement was for David to pay off his father's debt by working for Wilson at his roadhouse tavern for six months at about six dollars per month.

David described Abraham Wilson and the kind of establishment Wilson ran:

> ... my father ... informed me that he owed a man ... Abraham Wilson, the sum of thirty-six dollars, ... and if I would work out the note ... he would discharge me from his service, and I might go free. ... I set in, and worked with all

my might, not losing a day in six months. When my time was out, I got my father's note, and then declined working with the man [Wilson] any longer, though he wanted to hire me mighty bad. The reason was, it was a place [Wilson's tavern] where a heap of bad company met to drink and gamble, and I wanted to get away from them for I know'd if I staid [sic] there, I should get a bad name, as nobody could be respectable that would live there. [N, 45]

There was a societal expectation in the late 1700s and early 1800s that young males would contribute some of their earnings to the parents' household—and would sometimes work off a father's debts. In return for David's agreeing to a short indentureship to Abraham Wilson, John Crockett agreed to relinquish any paternal claims to David's future earnings. Beyond any filial responsibility David might have felt toward his father, the prospect of being forever free of financial obligation to John was undoubtedly a strong incentive for David.

Panther Springs History

Abraham Wilson's tavern was in an area known as Panther Springs, where a village had been established around an unusually large natural spring near the intersection of two main roads. From that crossroads, a route left the main Holston Road and went north along Panther Creek to the Holston River and then on to Bean's Station.

One of the earliest accounts of the Panther Springs settlement comes from 1799 in the records of Steiner and Schweinitz, two Moravian missionaries traveling from Salem, North Carolina. The missionaries gave their assessment of the land around John Crockett's and Abraham Wilson's taverns:

We passed through a region which because of its lack of water is known as the Pine Barrens.* The land looked poor, but we were informed that a fine plantation lying near an excellent spring, referring to the Panther Springs, was provided with a new two-story dwelling by its owner, who formerly lived four miles from Liberty in Lancaster County, Pennsylvania.

… this land is … fertile … Major Jackson of Philadelphia is here.[172]

*Note that "the Barrens" also referred to tracts of land where the Native Americans or early settlers had burned over large areas for cultivation or improved hunting. Those burn areas became overgrown with fast-growing pine and cedar trees as reforestation began to occur.

IB 37
PANTHER SPRINGS
½ mile along the Old Stage Road, a thriving pioneer community grew up around the enormous spring at which one Col. Bradley killed a panther. Panther Springs Academy was here. Tate's Store, also the post office, was the meeting place for the commissioners who created Hamblen County. In the spring are remains of an Indian mill.

---

172   Williams, *Early Travels in the Tennessee Country.*

Early Settlement of Panther Springs

The earliest settlement at Panther Springs was established between 1782 and 1783. John Evans, originally from Pennsylvania, was a well-to-do land speculator and owner of the respected Old Tavern. Evans was trading in East Tennessee land from 1790 through 1828, according to records in the courthouses in Rogersville and Rutledge Counties. In 1790, Evans partnered with a man named Jackson (another merchant and land speculator from Philadelphia) and bought lands on the north side of the Holston River, paying James Orr eight hundred dollars for the parcel. Three years later in 1793, John Evans acquired a substantial three hundred acres in Hawkins and Jefferson Counties on the south side of the Holston River at the head of Panther Creek. By David's account, the Panther Springs neighborhood spanned from the Abraham Wilson tavern on the west, across to the Quaker neighborhood of John Canaday at the east.

Panther Creek runs about five miles as the crow flies before it empties into the Cherokee Reservoir. Today, the land is preserved as one of Tennessee's fifty-six state parks: Panther Creek State Park, which is a 1,444-acre stretch in the historic Holston River Valley, is located six miles west of Morristown.

Abraham Wilson and a Village with Bad Character

Back in 1802 in the Panther Creek neighborhood, David had agreed to work for tavern owner Abraham Wilson in order to satisfy his father's debt of thirty-six dollars. The Old Stage Road connected Panther Springs, John Evans's Old Tavern, and Abraham Wilson's less-reputable roadhouse. In *Sketches*, Abraham Wilson and the character of his neighborhood is described as: "a merchant in a little village not too many miles distant, … The village had a bad character and David protested against going."[173]

The Ulster-Scots temperament on the frontier was rough and often

---

173   Clarke, *Sketches*, 33.

dissolute, and displays were common of drunkenness, promiscuity, gambling, fighting, spousal and child abuse, debt-dodging, and generally poor work habits. Many in the Ulster-Scots population were freewheeling and often engaged in high-risk land speculation and business ventures. Business failures were not uncommon, as could be attested to by John Crockett and others who had a hard time finding business success.

At this time and place, religion seemed to have taken a back seat to the gratification of more immediate needs. The holding of enslaved people was not uncommon; 1801 Morristown historical records noted that Old Town Tavern owner John Evans had given his son William: "a mulatto girl named Sal to possess [and] to hold ..."[174]

Even to a frontier lad like David, who grew up around his own father's rough kind of roadhouse, Abraham Wilson's tavern represented some of the worst aspects of early frontier character and people. After David cleared his father's debt to Abraham Wilson, he wasted no time in leaving Wilson's establishment in the fall of 1802. Crockett displayed a degree of maturity, character, and self-discipline in the way he worked to satisfy his father's debt. Crockett was reportedly so focused that he labored six straight months with no days off.[175]

Abraham Wilson's tavern in Panther Creek was located near the present-day outskirts of Morristown, near Brady Drive and the Old Stage Road, where one can pass by the sites of both the Evans and the Wilson taverns. Today the area is known as the Alpha neighborhood, sited between Jefferson City and Morristown near the Panther Creek State Park off US Highway 11E.

Living with the Quaker John Canaday

After six months of working for Abraham Wilson in an environment contrary to his values, David next took up employment with a Quaker, John Canaday. The Quaker families adhered to stricter codes of

---

174   WPA Transcriptions of County Archives. *History of Morristown 1787–1936.*

175   *Narrative,* 65.

conduct than those practiced by the Ulster-Scots. The Quakers' ethic fostered hard work as a part of daily moral and spiritual responsibility. It was quite the lifestyle change for David, going from life in a rough-and-tumble roadside tavern, now to living and working with a family of quiet and deliberate Quakers.

Sketches reported that David said that after he left the Wilson job and "hearing that the Quakers, many of whom resided in the village neighbourhood, ... were remarkable for their kindness" and "were famous for their workmanship" and he being "much in want of clothes," he went to work among them until he was "genteelly dressed."[176]

John Canaday agreed to hire David for a trial week. At the end of the week, Canaday was well pleased with the quality of David's work and brought him on. It was only then that David learned that John Canaday was yet another creditor owed money by his father: Canaday held a note on John Crockett for forty dollars. Canaday proposed that David work for him for six months to pay off his father's debt. At this point, David must have thought his father's debts were hiding under every rock in the county, which may have been the case.

Regarding this financial obligation to Canaday, David wrote in his *Narrative*:

> I concluded it was my duty as a child to help him [my father] along and ease his lot as much as I could. I told the Quaker I would take him up at his offer, and immediately went to work. I never visited my father's house during the whole time of this [six months] time.[177]

Canaday owned the land on which Crockett's tavern sat, so it's likely that Crockett's debt may have been incurred for back rent. Regardless of the debt's source, David voluntarily worked a total of

---

176 Clarke, *Sketches*, 34–35.

177 *Narrative*, 46.

twelve consecutive months for Canaday, without any personal income, to help pay off his father's debts.

Sketches offered insight into Crockett during this period: "In this part of his life, he has perfect recollection of never having failed to work a single day while in the employment of his old friend, the Quaker. It however served to give him a good character, and he never wanted for employment afterwards."[178] The influence of John Canaday on David was profound. Although David continued to do many things of which Canaday disapproved, they thought enough of each other to be sensitive and tolerant. John Canaday was a father figure for David—one quite different from his natural father. Canaday had a strong influence on David's character development.

Where John Canaday Came From

John Canaday had come to Tennessee at fifty-four years of age from New Garden Monthly Meeting (Quaker community) on Cane Creek in Guilford County, North Carolina.[179] The Canaday family arrived in 1796 and settled on the headwaters of Panther Creek near the Panther Springs village, on land purchased from William Spurgeon in 1795.

Until 1981, the identity of David's Quaker employer was unclear, with the Quaker's name given in Crockett's *Narrative* as *John Kennedy*. In his *Annotated Edition* of the *Narrative*, page 46, footnote 4, Folmsbee noted: "No information directly relevant to this person [Kennedy] has been found. There is, however, a record of an earlier debt to a Daniel Kennedy, clerk of the court, state of Franklin, dated May 26, 1787."

But then in 1981, an article on Crockett for *An Encyclopedia of East Tennessee*,[180] written by this author and H. P. Hamlin, identi-

---

178 Clarke, *Sketches*, 34.

179 William Wade Hinshaw, *Encyclopedia of American Quaker Genealogy* (Ann Arbor, MI: Edwards Brothers, Inc., 1936), 487.

180 Jim Stokley and Jeff D. Johnson, eds. *An Encyclopedia of East Tennessee* (The Children's Museum of Oak Ridge, 1981), 144.

fied "John Kennedy" as *John Canaday/Canady*, the Quaker patriarch residing in the Panther Springs neighborhood and a member of the Lost Creek Monthly Meeting of Friends. Spelling conventions were less consistent in Crockett's era, and the Quaker's name *Canaday* could be interpreted phonetically as *Kan' adee*, and spelled in variations like Kennedy, Canada, Kanaday, or Canady.

Life and Work Under Canaday

David wrote in his *Narrative*: "We [himself and another bound boy] commonly slept up-stairs, and at the gable end of the house there was a window. So, one Sunday, when the old man and his family were all gone to meeting, we went out and cut a long pole, and, taking it to the house, we set it up on end in the corner, reaching up the chimney as high as the window. After this we would go up-stairs to bed, and then putting on our Sunday clothes, would go out at the window, and climb down the pole, take a horse apiece, and ride about ten miles" to visit their girlfriends [*N*, 51].

Many of David's ideas of fun, "frolics, reapings, shooting matches, and all-night courting" were not looked upon favorably by Canaday. But it seems unlikely that the old Quaker would not have noticed a pole leaning against his house, which suggests he may have taken a "don't ask, don't tell" attitude toward the hijinks of his bound boys.

John Canaday's Wealth and Generosity

The cultural differences between the Quakers and the Ulster-Scots also manifested in the strong work ethic of the Quakers, which focused their efforts on productive tasks and kept them from wasting their time and money in pursuit of pleasures and pastimes, which were more common within the Ulster-Scots community.

The result of this work ethic can be seen in the size of the farms the Quakers acquired. John Canaday bought two hundred acres on his arrival in Jefferson County in 1795, from William Spurgeon for three hundred pounds. In 1802, Canaday added another tract of 185 acres, purchased from Christopher Hussey, a Quaker from Blount County. In 1808, Canaday received a grant for another 230 acres from the State of Tennessee, giving him a total of 615 acres.

Of Canaday's generosity with a later wedding present, Crockett wrote:

> At this time [David speaking of his marriage in 1806], my good old friend the Quaker came forward to my assistance, and gave me an order to a store for fifteen dollars' worth of such things as my little wife might choose. With this, we fixed up pretty grand, as we thought, and allowed to get on very well. [N, 67]

Fifteen dollars was no small change, and spoke to old John Canaday's regard for young David Crockett. The generous gift from Canaday ended up being the only wedding gift Crockett received, apart from the two cows given him by his in-laws.

Surprisingly, David ended up living with and working for the Quakers not for just six months, but for four years. David's time with the Canadays, from the age of sixteen to twenty, were formative years. John Canaday saw something in David and the gifts he gave David amounted to a lot more than fifteen dollars: the kindness and tolerance John Canaday and the Quaker community gave David provided him with a wider perspective on people. David Crockett was still an Ulster-Scots, but a changed one. It was with Canaday that David lived, worked, and received his only schooling. According to a Canaday family account, David's teacher was Charles Canaday, John Canaday's brother. "David Crockett came from John Canaday's farm to live with Charles and went to a school with him"[181] and from which he did not leave until he married.

Despite the forty-five-year age difference between David and the old Quaker, the two seemed to enjoy a close association. David's

---

181   Canaday, *The Canaday Family Tree*, 28.

references to *John Kennedy* in his *Narrative* referred to him as "an honest old Quaker" [*N*, 46]. In other places, David referred to Canaday as "my old friend, the Quaker" [*N*, 47].

The Long Hole Mill Site of John Canaday, Panther Creek.

Paying Off His Father's Debt

David recounted that he never visited his father during his first six months of working among the Quakers, even "though he lived only fifteen miles off."[182] In *Sketches,* Matthew St. Clair Clarke recounts: "Although within twenty miles of his father's, he [David] had not visited there for twelve months."[183] Even though David hadn't seen his father in a year, he was unfailing in his loyalty to his father and loyalty to his own word. David had worked long and hard to pay off the debt owed by his father first to Abraham Wilson, and later to John Canaday.

After David had cleared his father's debt with John Canaday, he "went to pay my parents a visit" on a particular Sunday evening. He'd been at his father's home for a little while before he handed the note to his father who was thinking it was sent from Canaday for payment.

David told his father that the note was not presented for payment, but was given as a gift from himself to his father, who "shed a heap of tears" [*N,* 46]. This gift must have touched John Crockett for him to openly break down in his son's presence.

182   *Narrative*, 46.

183   Clarke, *Sketches*, 34.

CHAPTER 11:

Love Life of the Young David Crockett

Much attention has been given to David Crockett's romantic interests, perhaps because he gives the process of finding a mate a lot of attention in his autobiography. For reasons of discretion, he says early in his *Narrative*, he leaves out the actual names of the young women he romanced. There was great public interest in Crockett's love life after the release of his *Narrative* in 1834. The public has a keen and timeless interest in the romantic lives of celebrities (as one can see in the enduring popularity of today's gossip tabloids), and David Crockett was certainly a celebrated figure of his time.

Amy Sumner

In his *Narrative,* David discusses his romantic pursuits of several women. His omission of their names led over the years to much speculation as to the identities of these women and left many folks barking up the wrong trees. David would probably be amused by that. His first love, a young Quaker girl named Amy Sumner, represented a forlorn hope for Crockett: she was one whom he could only watch from a distance and wish that circumstances had been different. Her name was not discovered nor published until this author wrote about her in an article for *An Encyclopedia of East Tennessee History*, published in 1981.[184]

David described how his romantic attraction to Amy Sumner, the half-niece of his employer John Canaday, occurred from the moment he laid eyes on her in the fall of 1803, when David was age seventeen and being schooled by Charles Canaday (son of John Canaday). Amy had recently come to live with the Canaday family in the Panther Springs neighborhood of Jefferson County, near today's Talbott community in Hamblen County.

The young Quaker woman had come from Surry County, North Carolina, where she had been part of the Westfield Monthly Meeting of Friends. It is possible that she committed some kind of social contravention against Quaker norms in her North Carolina community, for on November 22, 1800, an entry appeared in the records of the Westfield Monthly Meeting: "Amy Sumner of Chestnut Creek, disowned."[185] The reasons for this seemingly drastic measure were not specified, but Hinshaw's *Encyclopedia of American Quaker Genealogy* noted that reasons for being disowned from the Quaker community included "fiddling and dancing" and "deviation from plainness in apparel or speech."

The timeline of Crockett's *Narrative* supported that Amy came to John Canaday's household around the summer of 1803. She must have been an attractive young woman, as *Sketches* noted that David's tutor (one of the Canaday sons) was, "… visited by a female relation. She was pretty and fascinating, and David began to feel a little unhappy whenever she was absent." *Sketches* noted that Amy Sumner's beauty must have been highly appreciated, as in short order "she had an offer a [*sic*] marriage from a wealthy neighbour, which was extremely gratifying to her relation."[186]

Despite the competition, David says in his *Narrative* that he was

---

184   Stokley and Johnson, *Encyclopedia of East Tennessee History*, 144.

185   Hinshaw, *American Quaker Genealogy*, 969.

186   Clark, *Sketches*, 35–36.

present when Amy arrived in Panther Springs, and that he fell "head over heels in love with her." When he finally got up the wherewithal to talk with her, his "talk was not disagreeable to her" [*N*, 48]. Regardless of any mutual attraction, Amy told David that she had pledged herself to her half-first cousin, Robert Canaday, another son of Crockett's employer, John Canaday.

Amy was likely the daughter of Thomas Sumner, but her father could possibly have been Bowater Sumner or Caleb Sumner, they being the only Sumner families listed at the Westfield Meeting of Friends in North Carolina. One source notes that Amy was the daughter of Joshua and Sarah Cox Sumner.[187] All of these Sumner men were half-brothers of John Canaday, who all shared the same mother, Phebe Beals.

Robert Canaday received a license to marry Amy Sumner on the twentieth of January of 1806. Solomon Cox (whose land adjoined Canaday's) signed onto the marriage bond that Robert Canaday had taken at the courthouse at Dandridge, and Cox also served as a witness at the wedding.[188] David was in attendance at the Sumner/Canaday wedding, as he noted in his *Narrative*:

> At last, the son of the old Quaker and my first girl [Amy Sumner] had concluded to bring their matter to a close, and my little queen [later identified as Polly Finley] and myself were called on to wait on them. We went on the day, and performed our duty as attendants. [*N*, 50]

For Quakers at this time, it was frowned upon to *marry out*—that is, to marry someone from outside the Quaker community. Because tight-knit communities tended to be relatively small in number, Quakers

---

187   Letter from Thomas D. Hamm, September 25, 1994: "Amy was the daughter of Joshua and Sarah (Cox) Sumner, Joshua Sumner, was, as you have it, a half-brother of John Canaday."

188   Jefferson County Marriage Records, Jan 20, 1806, "Robert Canaday to Amy Sumner, witnessed Solomon Cox.

had their hands full in trying to keep family members from marrying too closely within their own families and bringing sanction for those who married too closely with their own kin. As this applied to Amy Sumner and Robert Canaday, Amy's grandmother was Phebe Beals Canaday Sumner, who was also the mother of Amy's intended, Robert Canaday. Put more simply: Amy Sumner was marrying her half-first cousin.

This close family relationship and wedding between Amy Sumner and Robert Canaday apparently brought scrutiny from the Quaker church within that same year. On November 29, 1806, Robert Canaday was called to appear before the Lost Creek Monthly Meeting of Friends, where he "offered a paper condemning his accomplishing his marriage contrary to discipline with his first cousin, which was accepted."[189]

Three years later, Amy requested to be joined in membership to the Lost Creek Monthly Meeting of Friends. According to the Women's Monthly Meeting minutes dated September 30, 1809, Amy "having been for some time under the care of friends," was accepted into the community.

Margaret Elder and Two Hundred Years of Marriage Bond Confusion

For over two hundred years, writers have (with what turned out to be misplaced certainty) identified Crockett's second love interest as Margaret Elder, daughter of David and Margaret Gordon Elder. Jefferson County court records noted that a *David Crockett* had taken out a marriage bond for a *Margaret Elder*.

Margaret must have been quite a catch, described as "… a tall buxom lass, with cherry bitten cheeks and luscious lips, mischievous

---

189 Lost Creek Monthly Meeting of Friends Minutes, May 20, 1797, to August 27, 1831, for Nov. 29, 1806.

eyes, and hands doubly accustomed to handling the spinning wheel or rifle trigger."[190]

David says in his *Narrative* that his unnamed second love came from a family living near them in the Newmansville area of Greene County, less than ten miles northeast of David's birthplace on the Nolichucky. David recalled: "I found a family of very pretty little girls that I had known when very young. They had lived in the same neighborhood with me" [*N*, 49]. The Elder family were also neighbors in that vicinity, which lent support to speculation that Margaret may have been one of David's love interests.

Further supposed evidence that David had wed Margaret Elder came from the marriage license filed at the courthouse in Dandridge, which read:

> State of Tennessee–Jefferson County: To any licensed minister of the Gospel or justice of the peace–Greeting: I do authorize and empower you to celebrate the rite of marriage between David Crockett and Margaret Elder and join them together as husband and wife. Given at my office in Dandridge, the 21st day of October 1805. J. Hamilton, Clerk.[191]

However, when identifying Margaret Elder as one of young David Crockett's love interests, an unlikely coincidence made what seemed like clear evidence turn into a dead end. As it turned out, this Margaret had no connection to our David Crockett. Margaret Elder in fact married David's first cousin, also named David, who was a son of John Crockett's brother, William Crockett.

John Crockett and his brother William both named their sons David (naming their sons after *their* father David). Considering that two

---

190   Michael Wallis, *David Crockett The Lion of the West.*

191   Jefferson County Marriage Records Book 1, Entry Number 526. The original license is in the possession of Margaret Vance Smith [1992].

cousins with the same name, being close in age, living in the same county of Jefferson, and using the same courthouse for things like filing marriage licenses, it is understandable how the life histories of the two cousins could be easily confused. The wild goose chase of believing our David Crockett had married Margaret Elder came about due to these similarities in the biographies of the two cousins.

For more discussion about the Elder family and a modern-day brouhaha over possession and ownership of the marriage license of Margaret Elder to David Crockett's cousin, see Appendix G.

Mary (Polly) Finley

David's next attempt at a romantic relationship finally bore fruit. In his *Narrative*, he wrote: "I concluded I couldn't do any longer without a wife; and so I cut out to hunt me one" [*N*, 49]. Having a wife as a partner was essential for success on the frontier. While the husband provided resources and protection, a wife handled tasks like cooking and cleaning, weaving and spinning and making clothes, and milking cows and churning butter. In addition to those duties, a wife bore children (in families that often had ten or twelve offspring), nursing them, caring for them during illness (where doctors were scarce), and educating them (where no schools were available).

David's desire for a wife led to some serious soul-searching, as he wrote:

> I began to think that all my misfortunes growed out of my want of learning. I had never been to school but four days, as the reader has already seen, and did not yet know a letter.
>
> I thought I would try to go to school some; and as the Quaker had a married son, who was living about a mile and a half from him, and keeping a school, I proposed to him that I would go to school four days in the week, and work for him the other two, to pay my board and schooling. … I had been

with him nigh on six months. In this time I learned to read a little in my primer, to write my own name, and to cypher some in the three first rules in figures. And this was all the schooling I ever had in my life ... [*N*, 49]

It was this desire to better himself through education that brought David to the person of Mary Finley. Going by "Polly" (a common nickname for "Mary"), Polly Finley turned out to be the love of David Crockett's life.

CHAPTER 12:

David and Polly's Life Together

Having been previously disappointed in finding a wife, Crockett writes:

> I continued in this down-spirited situation for a good long time, until one day I took my rifle and started a hunting. While out, I made a call at the house of a Dutch widow, who had a daughter who was well enough as to smartness, but she was as ugly as a stone fence. … [But] if I would come to their reaping, which was not far off, [the Dutch widow's daughter] would show me one of the prettiest little girls there I had ever seen. [*N*, 57–58]

We assume that the *prettiest little girl* to whom David would be introduced was his future wife, Polly Finley. Tracking down the identity of the cosmetically challenged daughter who introduced David to Polly presented a formidable challenge: find a widow of Germanic origins, who lived not far from the home of Polly Finley and her family, and who had a daughter near David's age.

Search for the Dutch Widow

In David's day, people of Germanic extraction were often referred to as *Dutch* (as in *Pennsylvania Dutch*), which was a linguistic corruption of the word *Deutsch* for "German." German immigrants, much like the Ulster-Scots in the earlier decades of settlement, formed tight-knit communities, within which they tended to marry. Marriage partners might even be selected from among the same group of families who had left the mother country together, migrated to America, and settled together. Even marriage between cousins within the same family was not unusual, influenced by proximity and familiarity, and having few other choices for mates in a time when people might never travel more than a dozen miles from their homesteads.

Neighboring Greene County, Tennessee, was home to a Germanic population that tended to be more concentrated than in the surrounding counties. Early Jefferson County was home to Ulster-Scots, Germans, English, Welsh, Irish, African, Italian, and French immigrants, indentured servants, and enslaved people. The Ulster-Scots and English were the most numerous of the groups, but many nationalities and ethnicities were represented.

In searching for a Germanic family that had at least one daughter with a widowed mother, a likely candidate would be from the Cluck family (also spelled as Kluch or Kluck, a name of Germanic origin). The Cluck farm bordered the Finley farm where Polly lived with her father, William, and the rest of their family.[192] Farm owner Peter Cluck's father, Henry Cluck, lived less than five miles from his son.

Henry Cluck had married Mary Ann Shumaker in Virginia in 1792. With the maiden name of *Shumaker*, Mary Ann was most likely also of German descent. Among their many children were daughters Mary and Catherine. By 1805, Henry Cluck had been dead for several years, leaving his Germanic (Deutsch or "Dutch") widow Mary Ann and

---

192   Jefferson Co Deed Book J, P. 89, Thomas Dinnel to Peter Cluck, 25 Jan 1809, 50 acres/$100, "Above the head of Dumplin Creek adj the Old Holston Path, Christopher Bradshaw: John Bryan. Witn Wm Bradshaw, Henry Cluck.

daughter Catherine living at home. Catherine was then age 20, about the same age as David, and would be familiar with the Finley family, as their brother Peter was Finley's neighbor.

Catherine Cluck would not marry her future husband, James Walker, until September 20, 1806; so in 1805, she was likely still living with her mother, "the Dutch widow." It's likely then that Catherine Cluck was person who first introduced David to his future wife, Polly, at the reaping (harvest festival) in 1805.

Born January 4, 1787,[193] and a year or so younger than David, Polly proved to be all he hoped she would be. In his *Narrative*, he wrote: "I must confess, I was plaguy well pleased with her from the word go. She had a good countenance, and was very pretty ..." [*N*, 59]. David goes on to say of it, "We continued our frolic till near day. ... I had not often spent a more agreeable night" [*N*, 60]. Frolics generally entailed fiddle music, dancing, and drinking, as well as games and plays for children.

David and Polly: Lost in the Woods

After their introduction, David's courtship of Polly began. He tells of his participation in "a wolf hunt, where a great number of men were to meet, with their dogs and guns, and where the best sort of sport is expected. ... I had to hunt in a strange woods, and in a part of the country which was very thinly inhabited." David went on to write that the sky clouded up and he got himself lost.

David explained that when a young hunter gets lost, nine times out of ten he will strike out in the wrong direction—and that is precisely what David did. "I went ahead, though, about six or seven miles, when I found night was coming on fast; but at this distressing time I saw a little woman streaking along through the woods like all wrath." The

---

193   Daughters of the Republic of Texas Lineage Book Committee, *Founders and Patriots of the Republic of Texas* (Austin, TX: Daughters of the Republic of Texas, 1963), 470. Found in an account from the Flowers family.

little woman turned out to be Polly, who was also lost, having been out all day looking for her father's horses.

David was delighted, writing: "I would have taken her up, and toted [carried] her, if it hadn't been that I wanted her just where I could see her all the time, for I thought she looked sweeter than sugar; and by this time I loved her almost well enough to eat her" [*N*, 63].

David and Polly followed a path that led to a house where they stayed the night. "I set up all night courting; and in the morning we parted. She went to her home, from which we were distant about seven miles, and I to mine, which was ten miles off" [*N*, 62–64].

Only two map points are 1) seven miles from Finley Gap, and 2) ten miles from Panther Springs. One is about two miles northwest of the village of Mossy Creek and the other is between Dandridge Crossing (White Pine) and Leadvale. It is not likely that David and Polly were each lost in the Mossy Creek area, as it would have been well-populated. The Leadvale area, on the other hand, would have been quite thinly populated and near enough to David's description to be a likely area for the circumstances of the meeting. This area is near the point where the Nolichucky River intersects the French Broad River.

A Similar Story from the Tales of Daniel Boone

Again, a David Crockett story has a close parallel to a story told by Daniel Boone. The Boone story tells about Rebecca Bryan, Boone's future wife, who was out searching for her father's stray cattle when night caught up with her. Trying to find her way home in the dark, she followed a creek. Young Daniel Boone and a friend were deer-hunting at night, using a torch to find their prey (a practice called *firehunting)*. Rebecca saw the light from the torch and went toward it. Boone, suddenly seeing two eyes shining in the torchlight, quickly raised his rifle to shoot. Before things when horribly wrong, Daniel realized that the eyes were not placed right for a deer's eyes, and he paused for a fateful second. Seeing a rifle pointed at her, Rebecca ran in terror. Boone caught up to her and, putting her at ease, discovered the woman he knew he'd marry. John Mack Farager, a Boone biographer, calls this episode "boilerplate American folklore."[194]

As Farager says of the Boone story, a number of writers have speculated about the verity of Crockett's account of meeting Polly in the woods, saying it's too coincidental for David and Polly to each have found themselves lost, at the same time, and in the same place. Other authors have also found it hard to believe that a hunter and woodsman of Crockett's caliber could get lost in his own country, only ten miles from his home. It may be folklore, as Farager says, but given Crockett's record for being proved truthful in this examination of the *Narrative,* I think there is reason to not totally discount it as fiction.

The Trouble with Jean Finley

David met Polly's parents, and initially hit it off with her mother, Jean Finley, who was playful and seemed to encourage David's interest in her daughter. In fact, Jean seemed to have a general interest in lining up potential suitors for her daughter, and considered David one of several prospects. While Jean Finley may have considered David Crockett as one of many candidates for her daughter's affections, from David's point of view, his courtship of Polly Finley was an all-out effort. He was quite smitten with Polly. Though things started out well, David's courtship became much more difficult because of Polly's mother. On his second trip to Finley Gap to court Polly, her mother, at first encouraging, began an all-out effort to bar David from seeing Polly.

David discussed his troubles with Jean Finley in some detail. It is possible that Jean did some investigation into the character of David and his family, and came to a conclusion that he might not be a favorable match for her daughter, of whom she was obviously proud. Though initially encouraging of David's attentions toward Polly, Jean's attitude toward David turned to one of flat-out intolerance.

---

194   John Mack Farager, *Daniel Boone: The Life and Legend of an American Pioneer* (New York: Henry Holt & Co., 1992), 43–44.

David attributed her "wrathy" nature to her being "Irish." It is not clear if David considered Jean Finley as from *native Irish* extraction or Scots-Irish, even though David also described his own father as of "Irish descent," although the Protestant Ulster-Scots were of different character from the Catholic Irish.

Jean's temper was spirited and her nature gregarious. Later, after some time elapsed in courtship, David describes his all-out battle with Jean for her daughter's hand: "When I broached the subject, she looked at me as savage as a meat axe. ... I hadn't been there long, before the old woman as good as ordered me out of her house ... her Irish was up too high to do anything with her, and so I quit trying" [N, 64].

As David presented his character in his *Narrative*, he was clear about his fondness for frolics, drinking, and gambling, though all seemed to be within the bounds of normal behavior for someone of his age, in that time and place. It is possible that Jean began considering the unsavory nature of the neighborhood of John Crockett's tavern (as "a place of bad character"), coupled with the low-end nature of the accommodations and the associates of David's father (Abraham Wilson, for example). These factors may have raised a red flag in Jean Finley's mind, leading her to think that Crockett came from potentially bad stock, and may not be an acceptable choice as a son-in-law.

Polly's father, William, seemed to have no problem with David, however, and treated him "very clever" [N, 64]. Jean, though, fought the budding relationship to the very end, and conceded only when it became clear that Polly would marry David, with or without her blessing. Jean was apparently persuaded by William that alienation from their daughter would serve no useful purpose. Jean eventually relented when it was clear that she could not stop the relationship between David and Polly.

The Wedding

Within a year, David and Polly made their plans to marry. David felt confident enough in getting Polly to marry him that he set out on the fifteen-mile trek to the courthouse at Dandridge with his friend Thomas Doggett to obtain a marriage bond/license. The marriage license taken out by David for Polly Finley was attested by Thomas Doggett as David's bondsman. The Doggett family lived on land extending to the southeast of Morristown. Two sons of Jesse Doggett were Thomas and Miller Doggett. In the 1850 census for Jefferson County, Tennessee, entry #211, Thomas Doggett is listed at sixty-four years of age, the same age David would have been then. The Tennessee-born farmer's land was valued at twelve hundred dollars, and the census record noted that his household included his wife, Lucinda, age forty-seven, and son, Lasensy Simpson Doggett, age seventeen.

On Tuesday, August 12, Joseph Hamilton, Clerk of the County Court, issued him a marriage bond to wed Polly Findley (Finley). Hamilton was the same clerk who just ten months earlier on October 21, 1805, had issued a license for David's first cousin, also named David, to marry Margaret Elder. David could sign his own name by age nineteen, as evidenced by his signature on the license to marry Polly Finley dated August 12, 1806.[195]

---

195   David Crockett to Polly Finley, Marriage Bond, Jefferson County Courthouse, Dandridge, Tennessee, dated August 6, 1806.

The bond, which was required of every swan who was about to launch out upon the sea of matrimony, is still on file in the county clerk's office at Dandridge, Tennessee.

A detail of the Crockett wedding has survived and was reported by Mrs. Foy Quarles (on whose farm rests the site of William Finley's grave). One of Mrs. Quarles's ancestors was Thomas Galbreath, who partnered with John Crockett in their ill-fated mill venture. According to Mrs. Quarles, Galbreath's son Mahlon was at the wedding and was noted as a local prize fighter. Coffee was a rarity in those days and some was served at the wedding event. Mahlon put a twist of chewing tobacco into a cup of coffee that he handed to David, who sipped it with a predictable reaction.

David and Polly at Finley Gap

After their wedding, David and Polly settled for a time in the quaint rural setting of the old Finley neighborhood. This landscape includes the old neighborhoods of Long Creek and Finley Gap. The Long Creek portion of this old settlement area is visible daily to thousands of travelers and commuters: the junction of Interstates 40 and 81 is on land that was once a part of the southern boundary of these neighborhoods.

The farm of Crockett's friend James Blackburn was located on the southeast side of the interstate junction. Crockett and Blackburn became lifelong friends when David lived in this neighborhood; Crockett visited there many times from his marriage in 1806 through his trips from West Tennessee, heading to Congress in the late 1820s and early 1830s.

On top of Bays Mountain, where a group of ridges rise high above the interstate junction, was the home of James McCuistion, whose farm adjoined that of his friend and neighbor William Finley. The Finleys' home was seated right in the gap at a fine spring near the base of Bays Mountain. His farm reached down into the Dumplin Valley at a place known, appropriately, as Finley Gap.

Home of the Blackburn Family

It has been generally accepted in Jefferson County that when David and Polly chose their new rented home, it was located close to the home of the Finleys. The account in Crockett's *Narrative* does not give any clues as to its location, but the *Sketches* account would seem to indicate that Crockett was living very close to "his wife's mother." Crockett noted that when leaving his father's house after his marriage, he "then went back to my new father-in-law's" and "rented a small farm and cabin."

A letter written in 1884 by John Jacobs, an established Finley neighbor, tells us that "Crockett was a poor man when first I saw him. He was then a married man, lived three-forths [*sic*] of a mile from my father in Findley's [*sic*] Gap, in Bays Mountain, Tenn" (see Appendix H for the full body of the Jacobs letter). This credible reference establishes David's residence in what we know today as Finley Gap. The area is traversed by what is today the Chucky Pike, and defined by the Dumplin Valley Road on the north and the top of Bays Mountain on the south (where Hinkle Road intersects the Chucky Pike). Later accounts from 1902, 1927, and 1958 all indicate that David was living in the same neighborhood as the Finleys. Court documents are scarce, but at least one would link David with other residents of the neighborhood.[196]

According to the late Curtis Frank, a lifelong resident of Finley Gap, his maternal grandfather, Andrew Jackson Woods, had told him that David moved a cabin from its original site (at what is now 139 Chucky Pike in Jefferson City, Tennessee) to the spot where Mr. Frank's house was in the 1980s (now gone). This location is accessed today from the Dumplin Valley Road, but the old gap road ran right past the Frank house. He was sixty-eight years old when this author visited him on June 11, 1979, and was born in the old log house he believed belonged to Crockett. The credibility of Frank's account is aided by the information in the Caton 1958 newspaper article, which noted that the cabin of David and Polly was "just up the Dumplin creek road" from the Finley home. By 1958, the road had changed and the Frank house was "just up the Dumplin Creek Road."

Curtis Frank had a picture barely showing a corner of the old log house, with the notches square and pegged. I photographed the log crib. The old cabin was made of oak logs, two story, two rooms down and one up. The larger of two chimneys would hold a four-foot log in the fireplace. The house faced north with a large brick chimney on the east side, window in the logs upstairs, one window on the east side of the front door downstairs, and a window in the west end toward the front. There was a one-story addition connected flush with the west side and extending just past the halfway point of the two-story section which contained the kitchen and a small brick chimney on the south end, and a board roof.

Former owners of land on or around Mr. Franks's property: W. A. Frank; A. J. Woods; Simon Marshall; William Bettis; James Churchman; Samuel Collier; Rebecca and David Marshall; John Bryan; Reuben Churchman; Eli Bettis; Geo. W. Jones; Widow

---

196   "Robert Henry Hynds." *The American Historical Magazine*, Vol. VII, no. 1, January 1902, p. 298.

This old barn was located on the Finley farm and was in use at the time of Crockett's residence with the Finleys. Redrawn by artist Amy Campbell

Jacobs; Benoni Kimbroughs; James Sherrod; Geo. Gordon; and Wm. Bradshaw.

Curtis Frank also indicated that there was, on the property of Lottie Collier who lived at Collier's Crossroads, "a beech tree with Crockett's writing on it." The story of the tree marking is also supported by an account from 1902, which states: "The citizens of Long Creek point the stranger with pride to a tree he [Crockett] topped while living there." This reference indicates that the tree incident may have been common knowledge to many in that neighborhood for a long time after the departure of David from the community.[197]

In an account marked *October 1927* (from a local newspaper) is the following excerpt:

Crockett's Mountain Romance

AN AGED CUCUMBER TREE AND A LOG BARN

---

197   Jefferson County Will Book.

MARKING THE SCENE OF DAVY'S BACKWOODS
WEDDING TO LITTLE POLLY FINDLEY ARE STILL
STANDING

From Mr. Collier also I learned how, David Crockett left
the marks of his hatchet on a cucumber [beech] tree for all
the world to see. The story as William Bettis told it to his
grandson is this:

A neighbor one day discovered David Crockett chopping on
a tree just above the spring heretofore mentioned.

"What are you doing that for?" he asked.

Davy went on chopping as he answered:

"I am doing this for the memory of Davy when he is dead
and gone!"

Just above the spring, I found a cucumber tree with two
chopped places, which have caused part of its center to decay
so that the trunk is hollow. Tradition leads me to believe that
this can be none other than the tree upon which Davy was
chopping when he answered the neighbor's question.

Accompanying this article on a sheet of notebook paper was the
following undated, handwritten note by Imogene Horner: "The man
at the tree is Dowe Collier, my grandfather. The house is still standing
and is occupied by Mr. and Mrs. Clyde Brooks and daughter Clydie
Gail. Part of the barn is still standing but not in use. The barn and the
cucumber tree is on the farm I live on. The tree still shows the places
cut on it by Mr. Crockett." Mrs. Horner said that she had written the
account for a school project, with the date of the note being around
1946 or 1947.

Dr. Estell Muncy, in his book on Jefferson County, presented a picture of an old cabin with the caption, "Davy Crockett and Polly Findley's honeymoon cabin." He goes on to say, "This cabin in Findley's Gap was perhaps Billy and Jean's (Finley's) first home. For certain, it was the honeymoon house for David Crockett and Polly Findley in 1806."[198] The same cabin picture has been found elsewhere and said to be the Crockett honeymoon cabin and it was supposed to have been located on the Mansfield Gap Road across the road from the Mansfield Gap Church, only a short distance through the woods from the known Finley residence. This location is also in close enough proximity to have been David's rented farm property and/or the honeymoon cabin.

In total, these references provide sufficient evidence to establish Crockett's residence somewhere in the vicinity of the Finley home.

David and Polly's Home Life

Polly and David had two sons while living in their rented home in Finley Gap. The first was John Wesley Crockett, born July 10, 1807, and the second William F. Crockett, born November 25, 1808. It is likely that they named the children for David's father and Polly's father, respectively. William Finley would be a fine namesake for the Crockett's younger son William, having proved himself an ally to David, taking on his cause from the first and serving as an important intermediary between David and Jean, Polly's wrathful mother. The protective attitude of Polly's mother and her father's willingness to travel with them to their new home hundreds of miles away would indicate that Polly was a special daughter to them both.

Crockett's desire to provide for his family led him to odd jobs. In the spring of 1808, he worked at least one job as a bondsman, along with John Smithy, signing a bond executed by Jefferson County Sheriff James Bradford to guarantee the presence at court of one John Rouden

---

198   William Elder, Jefferson County records as a juror on July 30, 1797.

(who was being sued for damages of four hundred dollards for a debt owed to Robert Obarr and the Campbell Martin Company). The original contract appeared to be made to Obarr who was either an agent of the Campbell Martin Company or transferred his interest in the debt to them. The Campbell Martin Company was apparently owned by "Arthur L. Campbell, Hugh Martin, and Charles F. Keith of Jefferson County." The plaintiff said that Rouden "for value received promised to pay Robert Obarr or order four hundred bushels of good sound merchantable corn delivered at Thomas Reece's mill."[199] Attorney for the plaintiff was "Charles F. Keith" and for the defendant was "Parsons." A jury of Jacob Cluck, Argyle Taylor, William McBroom, James Hill, John Hill, John Edmunds, James Jameson, Williston Talbott, Leeroy Taylor, Edward Humpston, James Simpson, John Morris, and John Hayes convened at the courthouse in Dandridge on the third Monday of July 1809, and found in favor of the defendant Rouden. The proceedings were recorded by Joseph Hamilton, clerk, and D. Barton, deputy clerk.

From the files of Rev. Reuell Pritchett, historian of Jefferson County in the 1950s, comes the note of the great-great-grandfather of Frank and Fred Quarles, Field Billy Lions: "He [David] owned seven of the most vicious bear dogs in the South." We know from many other accounts about Crockett's fondness for bear hunting. In the conversations recorded by painter John Gadsby Chapman, David discusses the kind of hunting dogs he wants to have pictured in the painting to make it look authentic.[200]

Oral history from residents of the Finley Gap area indicated that stories about Crockett have been associated with the Spring Creek area of the county on the "old road up Spring Creek between hills past the old cheese factory there was an old log cabin stood in front of where Bush Lemons' house now stands." This area is about "eight miles east

---

199 Jefferson County Will Book 1, p. 82–84. J. A. Dunn, *The Knoxville Journal*, c. 1898, Crockett Biography File, McClung Collection, Knoxville.

200 Hauck, *Davy Crockett: A Handbook*, 14.

of Dandridge." Mr. Charles Bush Lemons said his grandfather, John Alley, told him that David Crockett had traveled past the old cabin many times and had stayed the night there. The route to Dandridge from Finley Gap probably came down the Spring Creek road.[201]

David's Account of Marriage to Polly

In his *Narrative*, David's account of his life after his marriage is quite brief:

> Having gotten my wife, I thought I was completely made up, and needed nothing more in the whole world. But I soon found this was all a mistake—for now having a wife, I wanted every thing else; and, worse than all, I had nothing to give for it.

> I remained a few days at my father's, and then went back to my new father-in-law's; where, to my surprise, I found my old Irish mother in the finest humour in the world.

> She gave us two likely cows and calves, which, though it was a small marriage-portion, was still better than I had expected, and, indeed, it was about all I ever got. I rented a small farm and cabin, and went to work; but I had much trouble to find out a plan to get any thing to put in my house. At this time, my good old friend the Quaker came forward to my assistance, and gave me an order to a store for fifteen dollars' worth of such things as my little wife might choose. With this, we fixed up pretty grand, as we thought, and allowed to get on very well.

> My wife had a good wheel, and knowed exactly how to use

---

201   Charles Bush Lemons, Visit March 20, 1980.

it. She was also a good weaver, as most of the Irish are, whether men or women; and being very industrious with her wheel, she had, in little or no time, a fine web of cloth, ready to make up; and she was good at that too, and at almost any thing else that a woman could do.

We worked on for some years, renting ground, and paying high rent, until I found it wan't the thing it was cracked up to be; and that I couldn't make a fortune at it just at all. So I concluded to quit it, and cut out for some new country. In this time we had two sons and I found I was better at increasing my family than my fortune. It was therefore the more necessary that I should hunt some better place to get along; and as I knowed I would have to move at some time, I thought it was better to do it before my family got too large, that I might have less to carry.

The Duck and Elk river country was just beginning to settle, and I determined to try that. I had now one old horse, and a couple of two year old colts. They were both broke to the halter, and my father-in-law proposed, that, if I went he would go with me, and take one horse to help me move. So we all fixed up and I packed my two colts with as many of my things as they could bear: and away we went across the mountains. [*N*, 67–69]

A slightly different account is given in *Sketches*:

I feel we shall not be able to relieve him [David] from the poverty which was ever his attendant; for we find him for two years after his marriage living with his wife's mother, and making barely enough for support. [*S*, 54]

Leaving Finley Gap

So in search of better opportunities, David and Polly left Finley Gap to move to Lincoln County on the Mulberry Fork of the Elk River late in the year of 1811 or perhaps the first half of 1812. According to the *Narrative*, they were accompanied by Polly's father who went along with an extra horse to help carry their accumulated belongings.

Samuel Bradshaw, born in 1782 and married in 1803, who lived in the same neighborhood as David and Polly, moved to Franklin County, Tennessee, the same county where David and Polly were living in 1812. Could one have moved there because the other did?[202] Or were there other neighbors moving there as well? These Ulster-Scots are well-documented as moving in groups to new lands and this appears to happen as they continued to follow the frontier west.

Polly Left Alone

Polly's ultimate fate, however, served to substantiate her mother's fears and intuitions. David's decision to leave Polly alone (for months at a time while he joined in the Creek War) left Polly far from the support of any friends or family—with three small children to care for. It is possible that this strain overcame her ability to cope under such adverse circumstances ... and resulted in her death on June 11, 1815—at age twenty-eight and after almost nine years of marriage, shortly after David returned from his second enlistment.[203]

David had been serving as a horseback gunman in the American army, fighting Creek Indians at Fort Strother and Fort Taladega, and later encountering British troops in the Florida campaign.

Of David's decision to leave his wife, small children, and new home, and go off to war, he wrote:

---

202 *Families of Jefferson County Tennessee 200 Years*. Ed. The Genealogical Society of Jefferson County, Tennessee, 1992, 7.

203 *Patriots of the Republic of Texas*, 470.

For when I heard of the mischief which was done at the fort, I instantly felt like going, and I had none of the dread of dying that I expected to feel. In a few days a general meeting of the militia was called for the purpose of raising volunteers; and when the day arrived for that meeting, my wife, who had heard me say I meant to go to the war, began to beg me not to turn out. She said she was a stranger in the parts where we lived, had no connexions living near her, and that she and our little children would be left in a lonesome and unhappy situation if I went away.

It was mighty hard to go against such arguments as these; but my countrymen had been murdered, and I knew that the next thing would be, that the Indians would be scalping the women and children all about there, if we didn't put a stop to it. I reasoned the case with her as well as I could, and told her, that if every man would wait till his wife got willing for him to go to war, there would be no fighting done, until we would all be killed in our own houses; that I was as able to go as any man in the world; and that I believed it was a duty I owed to my country. Whether she was satisfied with this reasoning or not, she did not tell me; but seeing I was bent on it, all she did was to cry a little, and turn about to her work. The truth is, my dander was up, and nothing but war could bring it right again.[204]

By his own words, David recognized the hardship he was imposing on his wife and children, but was driven by a hot-blooded desire to protect those under threat. He believed that going out and facing a threat before it showed up on their doorstep was the best way to protect his family and neighbors.

According to David, the great tragedy of his life was the loss of his

---

204 *Narrative*, 71.

wife, Polly. The unforgiving nature and daily hardships of early frontier life offered little time to do much more than survive, and usually only by back-breakingly hard work. In order to face down a threat before it showed its face at home, David left behind his family to go fight, over Polly's objections. The cause of her death is unknown, and some historians speculate that she may have been afflicted with either typhoid or cholera. Her illness in the summer of 1815 lasted several weeks.

When she died, David buried Polly on a hill near Bean's Creek in Franklin County, Tennessee.[205]

---

205   Wikitree, Mary Polly (Finley) Crockett (1788–1815), Accessed October 14, 2021.

CHAPTER 13:

Summary/Conclusion Crockett's Legacy and Life after 1812

Regarding Crockett's moral compass, some writers say that the historical David Crockett's failures far overshadowed his personal accomplishments and that his ambitions were unrealistic. The mythical Crockett, over time, successfully overshadowed his senior contemporary and fellow Tennesseean, Andrew Jackson, in popular culture. But where history is concerned there is a sharp contrast in their lives, politics, and careers.

Jackson's was the embodiment of the definition of history as "great accomplishments and terrible mistakes, heroic dedication and incredible cruelty." He was the hero of New Orleans and Horseshoe Bend, the architect of a new, popular, sovereign government and represented the surging power of the American frontier. But his ambition and plans dealt deplorably with the dispossessed Native Americans being ground up in the wheels of a government motivated by expansive self-interest.

All the negative components of this history definition are present in Jackson's Indian policies and the resulting Indian Removal Act of 1830. This action has been justly vilified as one of the most incredibly cruel political actions taken by the American government over its entire history. His program and its resulting consequences increasingly cast a shadow over the character and accomplishments of Jackson and his administration.

Indian removal was a primary plank in Jackson's bid for a second term in the White House. For that reason he took it very personally when a congressman from his own state opposed the plan. The process of Indian Removal that Jackson undertook was an evolutionary *next step* in the process of gaining full control of Indian lands. Jackson and his war secretary, John Eaton, played a game of *good cop/bad cop* with the Cherokees and other tribes as they both soft-peddled and strong-armed them into accepting what Jackson had in mind for them.

Indian removal as a tool of our sovereign government should be viewed, along with slavery, as one of the most incredibly cruel political persecutions undertaken by the American government over its entire history. This gross disregard for basic human rights increasingly casts a dark shadow over the accomplishments of Andrew Jackson and his place in history. Jackson alone is not to blame but he was the primary driver for removal—many had a hand in this long and tragic destruction of Native American culture.

David knew it was political suicide to buck Jackson on the Indian Removal Act. Not only was Jackson a vengeful and ruthless adversary, but Crockett's own constituents largely supported the bill. The was no incentive for David to oppose Jackson except for what David himself said about the act being unworkable and morally wrong. He could have voted his conscience with a quiet "no," but instead he persistently and publically opposed the bill's passage with his characteristic bullheadedness when knowing he was right. With this defiance David sacrificed his political career and ultimately set in motion events that would lead to his own death. Some have cast doubts as to the sincerity of David's efforts on behalf of Native Americans, citing his eagerness to fight in the Creek War in 1813. Subsequent publications cast David as the bigoted Indian hater as depicted in the Crockett Almanacs published after his death. But when one reads the Creek War section of the *Narrative,* it is not difficult to see that David had a clear vision of the realities of war and the often senseless cruelty of men charged with its prosecution. Commenting on Crockett's *Narrative,* John Gadsby Chapman, his portrait painter, relates:

> There were, moreover, many portions of his manuscript, cancelled by the counsel of his advisers, that gave him special vexation—chiefly such relating to inhuman massacres of Indian women and children, which, if he wrote of with half the intensified bitterness of reprobation that I have heard him express towards the perpetrators of such atrocious acts, an officials whom they were permitted, suppression may have been better for the credit of the nation and humanity.

Reading David's accounts of his Indian Campaigns, one would find it difficult to imagine worse scenes than those he describes.

David was being considered by the Whigs as their nominee for president in the 1836 election. That ended when the Jackson forces put forth a concerted effort, narrowly defeating him in his re-election to his house seat in 1835. David's chances for getting the nomination from the Whigs had he won his election were still slim because he, in characteristic form, told the Whigs that he did not agree with a large portion of their platform.

He was not an effective politician because of his independent character and his aversion to compromise, but he was never short of moral courage. He could never be controlled by a group of politicians but lacked the ability of Lincoln to control them. His dedication in his fight against Jackson and the Indian Removal Bill is a testimony to his moral courage just as his stand at the Alamo was to his physical courage.

Jackson required unquestioning allegiance and David's character and ego were too strong to be dominated by someone else—even iron-willed Andrew. Jackson clearly and correctly saw himself as a man of destiny. He had purpose and driving ambition that burned white hot inside him and by shear force of will pushed himself far beyond his own body's physical limits to achieve his perceived purposes.

David by contrast saw himself as the product of his heritage and not the creator of a new one. His self-concept and success were derived from the esteem of friends and supporters giving him an inner strength and belief in him. His wit and humor, along with his solid abilities as a frontier citizen, gained him the trust and support of his friends and neighbors. In the end the only way in which Jackson was able to subdue him was to overwhelm him with resources too numerous for him to counteract—the same tactic used by Santa Anna against him and his comrades at the Alamo.

Crockett's death at the Alamo vaulted him from national celebrity into the realm of a national hero for the ages. He became a symbol of a uniquely American character.

Crockett and Boone helped define the culture of adventure in a new land. They breathed in the air of a new wild and immense land. They could live on this land in a way that their European forefathers never dreamed of and they instilled a love of the outdoor life that lives and is appreciated even today. Hunting, fishing, hiking, and camping have been and continue to be part of the soul of the American experience. Crockett and Boone helped our ancestors and ourselves understand our need to reconnect with nature and the outdoor experience.

The *Narrative* stands out as a rare and distinctly different account in the midst of a varied group of rich American folklore and folktales. If the work and David have been misunderstood, it is out of a lack of faith in his motives and in the directness of his account. My examination of the account leaves me with the overwhelming impression that it is written honestly and directly—without guile or fabrication. David displays an admirable ability to charge straight at the issues and facts—he is direct. It is this very directness combined with wit that is so refreshing and so American. David is a straight shooter in every sense.

Surely David Crockett was a part of great accomplishments and witness to terrible mistakes and incredible cruelty. He truly represented the people of the western frontier in his independent, straightforward, plainspoken, irreverent manner.

David Crockett was a man of character cut from the same cloth as Twain and Lincoln. His love for the wilderness and feelings for Native Americans are close to those of Daniel Boone. He arose from the ranks of the most humble Scots-Irish common folk and became a national icon. He represented and represents America and Americans. He was a man who makes us all proud to say we are Tennesseans.

Tennessee should be proud of David Crockett. He rose to the great challenges of his life with a record that most men would be proud to claim, and his personal style helped to create a uniquely American identity and culture. His autobiography, read closely, portrays a man of character and integrity who emerged from the depths of poverty and obscurity, overcoming incredible obstacles on his way to becoming a national symbol of the uniqueness that is America.

Acknowledgments

I am not unlike the turtle on the top of a fence post—it is apparent I did not get there on my own.

In helping to make this book possible, I want to especially thank Jefferson County historian Bob Jarnagin, Hamblen County historian Jim Claborn, Crockett Tavern Museum site director Sally Baker, the late Cherel Henderson, head of the East Tennessee Historical Society, and Steve Cotham, head of the McClung Historical Collection.

To the late Anna Brooks, a lifelong resident of Finley Gap who lived on the old Finley home site and provided me with critical information for three decades.

Bob Jarnagin, Jimmy Claborn and Joe Swann

To a great group of Kentucky Rifle experts who taught and assisted me in the best practices of restoring guns made at the turn of the 19th century.

The late Curtis Frank, a longtime resident of Dumplin Valley, Jefferson County, Tennessee. In 1979, he provided details relating to the composition of the old Finley/Crockett neighborhood. My friend Lucy Mitchell joined us for an interesting discussion with Mr. Frank, who passed away less than a year later.

Mr. & Mrs. Jack Kenley on whose farm is housed the old Long Creek Cemetery in the heart of the McCuistions' and David Crockett's old neighborhood.

Ms. Treva Mathis of the Quaker Collection at the Guilford College Library, Winston-Salem, North Carolina.

Artist Amy Campbell and technology guru Troy Galyon were of immeasurable help in taking the book into the 21st century.

I would like to give a special point of recognition and thanks to the first editor of this book, Joe Jansen of RootBole Wordcraft, LLC. His patience, care and tireless effort cannot be overstated. Joe helped me take over four decades worth of research, observations, and thoughts and put them together for this book. His recommendation of Mission Point Press has helped set the tone and scope of this book.

In conclusion I want to express my gratitude to all family members who have supported me and allowed me to put in the time required to bring this to fruition. Son Will Swann and my wife, Rebecca, have been excellent proofreaders and consultants all along the way.

Bibliography

Alderman, Pat. *The Overmountain Men.* Johnson City, TN: The Overmountain Press, 1970.

Arpad, Joseph John. ed. *A Narrative of the Life of David Crockett of the State of Tennessee.* New Haven, CT: College & University Press, 1972.

Bentley, Elizabeth P. *Index to the 1810 Census of Virginia.* Baltimore: Genealogical Publishing Co., 1980.

Bible, Jean Patterson. *Bent Twigs in Jefferson County.* Rogersville, TN: East Tennessee Printing Co., Inc., 1991.

Bicentennial Diamond Jubilee Celebration of Jefferson City, 1901–1976, published in 1976.

Bivens, John. "Crockett Redivivus: A Painstaking Recreation of Davy's First Rifle," *Muzzle Blasts*, January 1989.

Blair, Walter. "Six Davy Crocketts," *Southwest Review,* 1940.

Blomquist, A. K. *Cheek's Crossroads Tennessee, Store Journal 1802–1807.* Baltimore: Gateway Press, 2001.

Blount, William, *The Blount Journal, 1790–1796.* Knoxville, The University of Tennessee Press, 1955.

Boher, Melissa. *Glory, Passion, and Principle: The story of eight remarkable women at the core of the American Revolution.* New York: Atria Books, 2003.

Bradley, Abraham. Maps of the U. S. Exhibiting Post Roads....Post Offices, Stage Roads, Counties and Principal Mines. 5th Edition, 1804. Library of Congress, Div. of Maps, G3700, 1804.b, B7a.

Brooks, Cora Davis. *History of Morristown 1787–1936.* Nashville, TN: Tennessee Historical Records Survey, Work Projects Administration, July 1940.

Brown, Jim, Forester, U. S. Forest Service. *The Timber and Vegetation of the*

Appalachian Region of East Tennessee and Western North Carolina in the Pioneer Period—1700 to 1850.

Burnett, J. J. *Sketches of Tennessee's Pioneer Baptist Preachers.* Nashville: Marshall & Bruce, 1919.

Canada, Charles M. *Canaday Family History.* Indianapolis, IN. Typewritten genealogy of the Canaday Family written prior to 1928. Copies furnished September 14, 1994, by Marilyn V. Harvey.

Challacombe, W. A. *The Benjamin Blackburn Family and Notes on Blackburns in America.* Carlinville, IL, 1942. Reprint, Mason, MI: Robert and Betty Peebles, 1988.

Clarke, Matthew St. Clair (probable author). *Sketches and Eccentricities of Colonel David Crockett of West Tennessee* (usual title). New York: J. & J. Harper, 1833. Reprint of *The Life and Adventures of Colonel David Crockett of West Tennessee.* Cincinnati: "For the Proprietor," 1833.

Cohn, Kathryn Coe. Letter, August 5, 1992.

Cohn, Kathryn Coe. Shared a copy of the Carter's Valley petition.

"Connie's Corner Odds and Ends," *Morristown Gazette*, September 4, 1962.

Crockett, David. *A Narrative of the Life of David Crockett of the State of Tennessee.* Philadelphia: Carey & Hart, 1834. Facsimile edition with annotations and introduction, ed. James A. Shackford and Stanley J. Folmsbee. Knoxville: University of Tennessee Press, 1973.

Crockett Tavern and Pioneer Museum, pamphlet.

Dandridge Homecoming '86 Festival Committee, Edited and Compiled by Jean Bible, Jewell Hodge, Mary Jo Henry. *Historic Dandridge Yesterday and Today*, 1986.

Daughters of the Republic of Texas Lineage Book Committee. *Founders and Patriots of the Republic of Texas.* Austin, TX: Daughters of the Republic of Texas, 1963.

Derr, Mark. *The Frontiersman: The Real Life and Many Legends of David Crockett.* New York: William Morrow Press, 1995.

Dobson, David. *Directory of Scots in the Carolinas.* Baltimore: Clearfield Co., 2009.

Doughty, Richard. *Greeneville: One Hundred Year Portrait (1775–1875)*, 1975.

Dunn, J. A. *The Knoxville Journal*, c. 1898, Crockett Biography File, McClung Collection, Knoxville.

Elder, Miles M. Letter to the Tennessee State Library, May 14, 1931. In possession of the Tennessee State Library, Genealogy Dept.

Families of Jefferson County Tennessee 200 Years. Ed. The Genealogical Society of Jefferson County, Tennessee, 1992.

Faragher, John Mack. *Daniel Boone The Life and Legend of an American Pioneer.* New York: Henry Holt & Co., 1992.

Floyd, Don. *Morristown Citizen Tribune,* June 23, 1968.

Ford, Henry Jones. *The Scots-Irish in America.* Princeton: Princeton University Press, 1915.

Galbraith, James Paul. "Galbraith Ancestry." Knoxville, TN, undated genealogical paper.

Givens, Lula P. *Christiansburg, Montgomery County, Virginia, in The Heart of the Alleghenies.* Pulaski, VA: Edmonds Printing, Inc., 1981.

Goodspeed, *History of Tennessee.* Nashville: The Goodspeed Publishing Co., 1886.

Greene County History Book Committee, *Historic Greene County, Tennessee and Its Peoples: 1783–1992.* Don Mills, 1992.

Hale, Will Thomas and Dixon L. Merritt, *A History of Tennessee and Tennesseans.* Lewis Publishing Co., 1913.

Hamblen County Centennial Committee. *Historic Hamblen, 1870–1970.* Morristown, TN, 1970.

Hamm, Thomas D. Letter, September 25, 1994.

Hauck, Richard Boyd. *Davy Crockett: A Handbook.* Lincoln: University of Nebraska Press, 1982 & 1986.

Helms, Margo. "Barton Springs; Davy Crockett Slept Here," *Morristown Daily Gazette,* November 13, 1966.

Hinshaw, William Wade. *Encyclopedia of American Quaker Genealogy.* Ann Arbor, MI: Edwards Brothers, Inc., 1936.

Hynds, Judge Alexander. "Davy Crockett. Something About the Famous Old Hero and His Rifle," *Louisville Courier Journal,* Monday morning, February 13, 1893.

Jones, Jesse A. "Say it ain't true, Davy! The Real David Crockett vs. The Backwoodsman in Us All," *Appalachian Journal,* Fall 1987.

Jones, Kathryn. *Crockett Cousins,* self-published, 1984.

Journal of Jefferson County Genealogical Society, Dandridge, TN, April 2010.

Kegley, Frederick Bittle. *Kegley's Virginia Frontier.* Genealogical Publishing Co., 1938.

Lemons, Charles Bush. Visit, March 20, 1980.

Library of Congress, Div. of Maps, G3700, 1796, B7a. From a map in the British Museum 591307--523.40, 3rd Edition.

Lusk, Charles W. *Chattanooga Times,* October 6, 1942.

Mathews, Maxine. *Old Inns of East Tennessee.* East Tennessee Historical Society Publications, 1928.

Morristown Daily Gazette Mail, July 21, 1949.

National Park Service. "Bison Bellows: Bison East of The Mississippi." https://www.nps.gov/articles/bison-bellows-9-16-16.htm.

NC Land Grants Recorded in Greene County, Southern Historical Press, 1981.

North Carolina Daughters of the American Revolution. *Roster of Soldiers from North Carolina in the American Revolution.* Baltimore: Genealogical Publishing Company, 1967.

Pension application of Robert Crockett, S30353. Southern Campaigns American Revolution Pension Statements and Rosters, https://revwarapps.org/s30353.pdf, accessed March 11, 2021.

"Petition of the Inhabitants of the Western Country," TnGenWeb Project website. https://www.tngenweb.org/pre1796/178712f.html. Accessed March 18, 2021.

Price, Glanville. *Languages in Britain and Ireland.* Oxford: Wiley-Blackwell, 2000.

Public Broadcasting Service, *Antiques Roadshow*, "David Crockett, Margaret Elder marriage license," January 2006.

Ramsey, J. G. M. *The Annals of Tennessee to the End of the Eighteenth Century.* Charleston, SC: Walker & Jones, 1853.

Rankin, Roy M. Jefferson County Historical Society Newsletter, Spring 2001.

Reynolds, L. W. "The Pioneer Crockett Family of Tennessee," *Daughters of the American Revolution Magazine*, April 1921.

"Robert Henry Hynds." *The American Historical Magazine*, January 1902.

Shackford, James A. *David Crockett: The Man and the Legend*, ed. John B. Shackford. Chapel Hill: University of North Carolina Press, 1956.

Shumway, George. "Long Rifles of Note," *Muzzle Blasts*, October 1980.

Siler, C. E. (Bud). Asheville, North Carolina. Letter dated September 10, 1990.

The Siler Family. http://www.sonsofdewittcolony.org/mckstorysylar1.htm. Website accessed April 25, 2021.

Smith, J. Gray. *Review of East Tennessee or A Brief Historical, Statistical, and Descriptive Review of East Tennessee, United States of America: Developing Its Immense Agricultural, Mining, and Manufacturing Advantages, with Remarks to Emigrants, 1842.* Reprinted by The Reprint Company, Spartanburg, SC, 1974.

Smith, Margaret Vance, Tampa, FL. Letter to Rick Farrar, County Clerk, Jefferson County, TN, dated February 19, 2010.

Southern Historical Research Magazine, November 1936.

Speer, William S. *Sketches of Prominent Tennesseans.* Nashville: A. B. Tavel, 1888.

Stokley, Jim and Jeff D. Johnson, eds. *An Encyclopedia of East Tennessee.* The Children's Museum of Oak Ridge, 1981.

Summers, L. P. *Annals of Southwestern Virginia 1769–1800.* Abingdon, Virginia, 1929.

Torrence, Robert and Robert L. Whittenburg. *Colonel "Davy" Crockett. A Geneaology.* Washington, DC: Homer Fagan, 1956.

University of Tennessee Special Collections Library Map identified as "Scott, P45212," titled S.W. Territory 1795.

University of Tennessee Special Collections Library Map identified as #912.768, State of Tennessee, 1795.

Wallis, Michael. *David Crockett: The Lion of the West.* New York: WW Norton, 2011.

Wigginton, Eliot. *Foxfire 5.* Garden City, NY: Anchor Press/Doubleday, 1979.

Wikipedia; Wikipedia's "Bibliography on Works on David Crockett," entry. Accessed January 4, 2021. https://en.wikipedia.org/wiki/ Bibliography_of_works_on_Davy_Crockett

Wikitree; Wikitree's "Mary Polly (Finley) Crockett (1788–1815)," entry. Accessed October 14, 2021.

Williams, Samuel Cole. *Dawn of Tennessee Valley and Tennessee History.* Johnson City, TN: Wautaga Press, 1937.

Williams, Samuel Cole. *Early Travels in the Tennessee Country.* Johnson City, TN: Wautaga Press, 1928.

WPA Transcriptions of County Archives. *History of Morristown 1787–1936.*

Additional Resources

Abbott, John S. C. *David Crockett: His Life and Adventures.* Los Angeles: Enhanced Media Publishing, 2017. First published in 1898.

Benge, Janet and Geoff Benge. *David Crockett: Ever Westward* (Heroes of History). Lynnwood, WA: Emerald Books, 2012.

Davis, William C. *Three Roads to the Alamo: The Lives and Fortunes of David Crockett, James Bowie, and William Barrett Travis.* New York: HarperCollins, 1998.

Groneman, William. *David Crockett: Hero of the Common Man* (American Heroes, 5). New York: Forge Books, 2007.

Levy, Buddy. *American Legend: The Real-Life Adventures of David Crockett.* New York: G. P. Putnam's Sons, 2005.

Lofaro, Michael, ed. *The Life and Adventures of Colonel David Crockett of West Tennessee.* Knoxville: University of Tennessee Press, 2020.

APPENDIX A:

Kings Mountain Combatants Associated with Crocketts

The following is a listing of some of the combatants at the October 7, 1780, Battle of Kings Mountain, who likely knew or were

Col. Geo. Gillespie
Maj. Walter Crockett
Capt. Jos. Crockett
Capt. John Fain
Capt. Thom. Gillespie
Capt. Wm. Gillespie
Capt. Ninnian Hoskins
Capt. James Roddy
Capt. John Snoddy
Capt. James Stinson
Lt. Wm. Crockett
Lt. Robt. McFarland
Lt. Adam Meek
Isaac Barton
John Blackburn
Jos. Blackburn
Robt. Blackburn
Wm. Brazelton
Thom. Brotherton
John Carson

John Crockett
William Crockett
Rev. Felix Earnest
Robert Elder
George Findley
John Findley
Arthur Galbreath
John Galbreath
Robert Galbreath
John Gass
Alexander Gilbreath
Preston Goforth
Abednego Inman
Arthur Inman
John Inman
Robert Inman
William Kindle
John Kitchen
Aquilla Lane
Tidence Lane

John McAdoo
Wm. McCallister
Adam Meek
Jas. Miliken
John Newman
Alexander Outlaw
Robt. Patton
Adam Peck
Francis Quarles
John Quarles
David Rankin
Wm. Rankin
James Reese
Jos. Stencipher
Geo. Stockton
John Stockton
William Stockton
Parmenas Taylor
George Turnley
Peter Turnley

associated with John Crockett, father of David Crockett.[206, 207]

---

206   Letter to the Tennessee State Library, May 14, 1931. In possession of the Tennessee State Library, Genealogy Dept. *Southern Historical Research Magazine*. Vol. 1, No. 5, Nov 1936, p. 476-477.

207   "Robert Henry Hynds." *The American Historical Magazine*, Vol. VII, No. 1, Jan, 1902, p. 298. William Elder, Jefferson County records as a juror on July 30, 1797.

APPENDIX B:

Chain of Land Ownership—Crockett's Tavern Site

Surprisingly, to date there has not been an exhaustive title search of the Morristown Tavern site property. According to Jim Claborn, Hamblen County Historian, the tavern property belonged to John Rice at the time of Hamblen County's establishment in 1870. Jefferson County records indicate that John Rice bought the property from William Poindexter in a fifty-acre tract on January 12 of 1842. Poindexter had acquired it from James Landrum on October 14, 1835, in a ten-acre tract that joined "Alexander Millikan's line."

Landrum had obtained it from Benjamin McFarland just two days earlier, on October 12, 1835, for two thousand dollars, as a part of a 408-acre tract with adjoining lines to Alexander Millikan, James Millikan, and William Evans, indicating that the tract was property upon which McFarland had resided.

McFarland had purchased this parcel of the property on April 6, 1815, in a tract from Quaker John Canaday, Sr., who was to become David's role model, trusted friend, and employer. The deed is witnessed by Elihu Millikan and William Line.[208] Coincidentally, William Line had been the high bidder for John Crockett's Mossy Creek land at the sheriff's sale back in 1795.

It is thus likely that John Canaday Sr. was the owner and landlord of Crockett's Morristown Tavern site.

---

208   Jefferson County records

APPENDIX C:

Quaker Names Associated With Crockett

Canaday, Charles—Father of Charles and John; b. ca. 1715
m. Phebe Beals, 1739, Prince George County, MD
d. prior to 1746 [Also see London County, VA, Fairfax Monthly Meeting]

Canaday, Phebe—b. ca. 1720, Chester County, PA
m. 1st Charles Canaday, 1739, Prince George County, MD; 2nd Robert Sumner, September 29, 1746, children: Wm., Bowater, Caleb, Joshua, Thomas, Robert, Prudence, Phebe, Abigail, Sarah

Canaday, Charles—Brother to John, Sr.; b. September 25, 1740, Frederick County, VA
m. Abigail Foster, daughter of Hugh and Abigail Foster, March 13, 1771
d. July 14, 1797, Guilford County, NC

Canaday (Kennedy), John, Sr.—b. April 5, 1741, Fairfax County, VA; Parents were Charles and Phebe Beals Canaday
   m. Margaret Thornbrough, daughter of Walter Thornburgh of Deep River Monthly Meeting, NC; b. ca. 1744 in PA; married April 10, 1764; d. March 12, 1819, Wayne County, IN (West Grove)
   d. March 2, 1830, Randolph County, IN (89 years old)

The Canadays located in North Carolina at Carvers Creek Monthly Meeting in Bladen County, at Cane Creek Monthly Meeting in Orange County, and then to New Garden Monthly Meeting.

Stepfather Robert Sumner was not originally a Quaker but became one after his marriage to Phebe.

On October 29, 1796, Robert left New Garden Monthly Meeting in North Carolina (Hinshaw, Vol.1, 530); May 20, 1797, and arrived at Lost Creek Monthly Meeting.

Canaday (Sumner), Phebe—Mother of John Sr.; remarried Robert Sumner; children of John and Margaret Canaday: Phebe, b. January 10, 1765; Henry, b. June 29, 1766, m. Matilda; Bowater, b. April 14, 1768, m. Mary; Charles, b. April 18, 1770, m. Sarah Russell, April 1794; Walter, b. December 19, 1771; John Jr., b. April 13, 1774, m. Jarlitha Cox, March 27, 1799; Robert, b. January 13, 1777.

Property Records
Bought:

C-297—6/22/1795, 200 acres SS of the Holston River from Wm Spurgeon for 300£. SS Holston River, North side of the knobs that divide the waters of the Holston and the French Broad rivers, "being the place where the said Spurgeon now lives." Witnessed Mordecai Mendenhall and Boater Kenedy.

"William Spurgin" had the land originally granted to him in Grant #1469 in 1789 from Sullivan County listed as 300 acres on the south side of the Holston River.

E-86—3/16/1799, 194 acres—$600—Job Cotton of Grainger County to John Kennedy "Opposite to the head of Panther Creek adj djoining William Spergan. Test Mordicai Mendenhall, Robert Kennedy. Approved in Court 3rd Monday in Jan, 1801, appraisers appointed were Bradshaws, Samuel West, Chas Kennedy & Pery Talbott."

F-192—5/5/1802, 185 acres, Holston River, from Christopher Hussey of Blount County, $500, "joining John Kennedy's land on the west side."

G-124—8/10/1803, 160 acres, NC Grant Book 5, p. 560.

J-70—9/13/1808, 230 acres, TN Grant #429—waters of Cedar Pond, Samuel Jackson's line, Soloman Cox's line, Chas Kennedy's line. This property is likely in the Finley Gap area as it is known that Solomon Cox and Samuel Jackson owned property there. The cedar pond and the maple pond are mentioned in the 1836 Jefferson County Civil District Survey here. One is called the Thomas Pond on recent maps and both were extant until sometime in the early 1990s when they went dry.

St of TN Grant #429-Book 1, p. 429—1/23/1809, 230 acres, Jeff Co.

St of TN Grant #429-Book 1-1, p. 469—1/23/1809, 230 acres, Jeff Co.

NC Grant Book 8, p. 387—8/10/1813, 160 acres, Jeff Co.

Sold:

Jeff Co Deed Book D p. 319—23 Oct 1798—G Fitzgerald to Geo Swingle 640 acres joining the lead mines. Test John Kennedy and Jos. Langdon.

Jeff Co Deed Book N p. 224–226—Deed from John Canaday, Senior to Benj. and Andrew McFarland on 26 April 1815. Witness Wm. Line-Elihu Millikan-Reg 20 May 1816. 86 acres for $86. NW of the ridge that divides the Chucky & Holston begin on dividing line between Canaday & Joab Patterson—line of Chas Canaday—w/Solomon Cox's line.

John Canady, Sr to Joab Patterson—June 28, 1814, Jeff Co Deed Book M, p. 25, "including the Long hole Mill and containing seven acres. Witness: Isaac J Watkins, Mordicai Mendenhall and Thomas Patterson. "Passing by a Cycam [sycamore?] on and running five feet into the water"—S56°W4P—S34°E1P—S65°W2P to the beginning. 125 acres; Reg 21 May 1815.

Jefferson County Misc Bonds: Bond #89, 14 March 1814, $500, James Kenady Decsd. Administrator: John Kenady; Security: John Kenady, John Lockhart, Jacob Peck. Signed by all above.

Crockett Tavern Property—Jefferson County records indicate that John Rice bought the property from William Poindexter in a fifty-acre tract on January 12 of 1842. Poindexter had acquired it from James Landrum on October 14, 1835, in a ten-acre tract that joined "Alexander Millikan's line" for thirty dollars.

Landrum had obtained it from Benjamin McFarland just two days earlier, on October 12, 1835, for two thousand dollars, as a part of a 408-acre tract with adjoining lines to Alexander Millikan, James Millikan, and William Evans, indicating that the tract was property upon which McFarland had resided.

McFarland had purchased this parcel of the property in a tract from Quaker John Canaday, Sr., on April 6, 1815. The deed is witnessed by Elihu Millikan and William Line. Was John Crockett's landlord on the Morristown tavern site John Canaday? That would help explain why Canaday had the note against Crockett which David agreed to work off for his father. This might also explain why David chose to go to Canaday to apply for work. He would likely have made his acquaintance prior to going to him in search of employment. Jefferson County Deed Book N, page 224. John Canaday, Sr. to Benj. & Andrew McFarland.

Canaday, Margaret Thornbrough—Wife of John Canaday, b. 1740

Canaday, [?]—Schoolteacher son of John Canaday from whom David Crockett took schooling for six months. *Narrative,* 49: "a married son who was living about a mile and a half from him and keeping a school." Could be Henry, Boater, Charles, Walter, or John Jr.

Canaday, Boater—Sept 9, 1815, sold 80 acres to Jacob Wilson, Attst Abraham Wilson. Son of John, Sr.
St of TN Land Grant #2254—6/9/1812, 130 acres, Bk 3, p. 394.
M-7—1814, Boater Kenedy from Francis M Aybury, 50 acres.

Canaday, Charles—Third son of John and Margaret, b. 1770.

Deed from Chas Canaday to Benj McFarland 6 April 1815.

Witness Wm Line-Elihu Millikan-p. 222–224. Reg 20 May 1816. 62 acres NW of the ridge that divides the Chucky & Holston.

Chas Kenedy Deed from John Lowe of Knox County 20 July 1798.

200 acres for 60£, waters of Holston River adj Christopher Hussey, witn John Kelly, John Caneedy, M Mendenhall. Jeff Co Deed Book D, p. 278.

Jefferson County Misc Bonds: Bond #20, 10 June 1811, $500,

Christeannia Morris Decsd. Adminestrator: Mordicai Mendenhall. Security: Charles Canaday, Mordicai Mendenhall. Signed by all above.

Canaday (Kennedy), George (*Am Hist Mag*. Jan 1902, Hynds, p. 298) A Rifle "… which Crockett gave to George Kennedy in part payment for a horse shortly after he was married to Polly Finley. Kennedy sold it to James McCuistion who left it to his son Maj. S S McCuistion who died suddenly in 1893. Hynds obtained it from Maj. McCuistion's estate."

Canaday, Henry—Deed to Thom Patton, Jeff Co Deed Book P, p. 102; Dec 7, 1815, 152 acres on Lost Creek.

Kenady, James—Jefferson County Misc Bonds: Bond #89, 14 March 1814, $500, James Kenady Decsd. Adminestrator: John Kenady. Security: John Kenady, John Lockhart, Jacob Peck. Signed by all above.

Canaday, Phebe—A daughter of John Canaday who married Mordicai Mendenhall and remained in Jefferson County when the others left. A continuing Jefferson County connection to the Canaday family.

Canaday, Robert—Jeff Co Marriage Records, Jan 20, 1806, Robert Canaday to Amy Sumner, witness Solomon Cox. Marriage Bond Jan 20, 1806, signed by Solomon Cox. First child born, Joshua, November 11, 1806.

Wm Burris to Eliz Bailey Jan 1, 1802, bnd Robert Canaday.

Canaday, William Sumner—According to Kathryn Coe Cohn, through the "process of elimination," this is John Canaday's school-teacher son.

Canaday, Walter—Jeff Co Marriage Records, "Walter Kennedy to Amy Huzy, Oct 8, 1796."

Cox, Solomon—Quaker Jeff Co Deed Book D, p. 211; 24 Mar 1798; Reg 21 June 1798; 100 acres, $40; Solomon Cox to Wm Cox "on the south side of the Holston River in the nobs joining the Barrens," "Beginning on Solomon Cox's line: N 55°E90P—S 75° E100P—thence 80 to a stake—thence W to Solomon Cox's line—thence along the same to the beginning." Witness Harmon Cox and Wm Cox; signed Wm Cox.

Jeff Co Deed Book J, P. 25; Jan 22, 1809; Reg Oct 13, 1809; 171 acres—From 1000 acres issued by Wm White to the heirs of John Cooper—171 acres assigned by John Brown & Jas Williams to Solomon Cox "in Honey Cut Valley adj his patented land on the west"—"on Harden's line."

Solomon Cox to Benj Cox—"P/A" Jeff Co Deed Book Vol R, p. 210—May 24, 1826, 2 Tracts

Cox, Joseph—Son of Solomon, m. Wm Line's oldest daughter Mary/Polly; moved to Indiana w/Quakers.

Ellis, Nehimiah—A Quaker. Attested Wm Crockett's deed 1794. NE witness with Abraham Woodward and Robert Pierce to will of Henry Thornburgh, 3/13/1804. NE witness with Abraham Woodward, Sr. to will of Joel Elmore. A NC Grant #1019 to Christopher Ellis Registered Nov 1, 1792, "Place he now lives on."

Frazier, Wm—Transferred from Center Monthly Meeting, NC, 1793.

Patterson, Andrew—Deed to Wm Golden, Jeff Co Deed Book R, p. 367; June 28, 1814; 7 acres.

Patterson, Jacob—Deed from Thom G Watkins, Jeff Co Deed Book L, p. 86; Feb 18, 1813; 230 acres.

Patterson, Joab—John Canady, Sr to Joab Patterson—June 28, 1814, Jeff Co Deed Book M, p. 25, "including the Long hole Mill and containing seven acres. Witness: Isaac J Watkins, Mordicai Mendenhall and Thomas Patterson. "Passing by a Cycam [sycamore?] on and running five feet into the water"—S56°W4P—S34°E1P—S65°W2P to the beginning. 125 acres; Reg 21 May 1815.

John Canady, Sr to Joab Patterson—June 28, 1814, Jeff Co Deed Book M, p. 84; 125 acres; Reg 21 May 1815, "Joining land belonging to said Patterson."

Reece, Yarnell—Married Davy's sister Betsy. From a Quaker family. Moved to West Tennessee and lived with David for a while there.

Sumner, Amy—b. ca. April 1782; m.; d. September 25, 1823, at age 41 David Crockett's first mentioned (but unnamed) girlfriend from the *Narrative*.

Amy Sumner was the niece of John Canaday who married Robert, a son of John Canaday. She had been disowned (Hinshaw, *Encyclopedia of American Quaker Genealogy*, 969, "11/22/1800 Surry County, NC—Amy of Chestnut Creek, disowned from the Westfield Monthly Meeting, NC"). Admitted to the Lost Creek Women's meeting September 30, 1809. Margaret Elder and David Crockett were attendants at the wedding of Robert Canaday and Amy Sumner. She was John Canaday's half-niece, the daughter of his half-brother.

Jeff Co Marriage Records, Jan 20, 1806, Robert Canaday to Amy Sumner, witness Solomon Cox. First child born, Joshua, November 11, 1806.

Amy Sumner's Story

The real second romance? Problems with the Margaret Elder story:

- It is 15.9 miles from Panther Springs to the Dumplin community—David Crockett says his girl lived ten miles away.
- David says he was eighteen at the time he was courting his second girlfriend—1786+18=1804—but the Quaker wedding took place in the fall of 1805–early 1806?
- The shooting match was on a Saturday and the wedding was to be on a Thursday.
- David's marriage to Polly took place in mid-August 1806.
- David Crockett—b. 1779, South Carolina, d. September 28, 1851, Gibson Co., TN

Sumner, Ed—Listed in Jeff Co Manumission Society

Sumner, Joshua—A chance this is the father of Amy. "In our history file we have a typed genealogy of the Sumner family prepared by George W. Moore in 1965 in which he states that JS had 10 children and moved to the Lost Creek Meeting ... where he lived to be over 100 years old ... one son Thomas"—From Guilford College Library Carole Treadway 3/28/1979. Possibility he was a brother to Amy.

Sumner, Robert—d. December 1, 1779. Stepfather of John Canaday.

Children of Robert and Phebe (Canaday) Sumner:

Wm., Bowater (1749), Caleb (1751), Joshua, Phebe, Thomas (1757), Prudence, Abegail, Sarah, Robert Bowater, Caleb, and Thomas were all at Westfield where Amy was.

Sumner, William—d. September 2, 1801

Jeff Co Court Minutes Sept 12, 1801, p. 35, William Sumner's Will was proven, Admns Isaac Hammer and Eleader Sumner. Will Book #1, p. 38, WS Will—Wife Eleder, daughter Phebe, friend Isaac Hammer; attest Jos Turner & Asa Mills.

Jefferson County Deeds Vol. E, p. 178—NC Grant #770—Walter Turner, 21 Jan 1797, 300 acres, Hawkins County nearly adj Wm Sumner on South and John Maulsbyon east, adj _____ Howard.

Adj Isaac Hammer—A-255.

Marriage Records

Robert Kennedy to Mary Russell—December 19, 1796

Walter Kennedy to Mary Huzy—October 8, 1796

John Canaday to Jarlitha Cox—March 27, 1799

Robert Canaday to Amy Sumner—January 20, 1806

APPENDIX D:

Data Sheet on Crockett/ McCuistion/Swann Rifle

- Overall Length—60¼" (likely 62¼" when made)
- 44" swamped barrel (originally 46" long—2" was cut off at some point). A swamped barrel is wider at the breech and the muzzle, but tapers toward the center of the barrel. A swamped barrel cuts down on weight while strengthening the pressure points where the powder explodes beside the lock, and where the bullet leaves the barrel at the muzzle.
- .488-caliber, seven-groove rifled octagonal barrel is 15/16" across the flats at the breech and is 1-1/16" across the flats at the muzzle. It is likely that 1" was cut off the muzzle and the breech at some time because of the stress wear and tear on those points.
- Weight: 10.1 lbs.
- Butt Plate 1¾» at widest point by 4⅝" high
- Pull length (Butt to trigger) of 14¼"

APPENDIX E:

Two David Crocketts

William Crockett, born ca. 1748, Davy's uncle, was likely the firstborn son of David and Elizabeth Crockett (Davy's grandparents). At the time of the Margaret Elder marriage license, William lived in the Dumplin community and had a son named David (b. 1779) who married Margaret Elder, and a sister to Drucilla Elder (1797–1842) who married David B. Crockett (another first cousin and a son of Davy's, a son of Robert Crockett). This Margaret Elder Crockett (married to Davy's first cousin David [son of William] b. 1779) received $1 from the proceeds of the estate of John Crockett who died in Gibson County, Tennessee, in 1834, leaving an infant. Davy Crockett was the administrator of the estate. Likely the deceased John Crockett was a brother to Davy.

David's uncle William Crockett lived in the Dumplin community where most of the Elders lived. On February 2, 1794, a deed was issued from William Goforth to William Crockett for one hundred acres "on the south side of Dumplin Creek and branch."[209] The property was sold for fifty pounds and attested by Alexander Shadden and Nehimiah Ellis. Among the earliest settlers "on the north bank of the French Broad above Dandridge were Benjamin McFarland, Hugh Kelso, Reverend Robert Henderson, Parmenas Taylor, William Moore,

---

209   Jefferson County Deeds, Volume B, page 46.

George Willcoxon, and William Goforth."[210] The area of habitation of Goforth, Willcoxon, and William Crockett was toward the mouth of Dumplin Creek near what is today the Jefferson-Sevier County line, Douglas Dam and the little community of Dumplin.

From the Dumplin Creek Baptist Church records, "Rebeccah Crockett," "Elizabeth Crockett," "Hannah Crockett," and "Margrit Crockett" are listed as some of oldest members of the church. These are likely daughters or daughters-in-law of William Crockett the elder. A "Margaret Crockett" listed as a charter member of Dumplin Baptist Church, July 30, 1797, was likely the wife of David Crockett, son of William. Isaac Newman, an early resident of the Mossy Creek area had a son, Robert, who is said to have married a daughter of Davy's uncle William named Margaret.[211] It is said that she grew up with Robert. No male Crockett names are listed.[212] It seems that David's mother was likewise alone in joining the church in the community of the tavern and it may indicate that the Crockett males were not known to be churchgoers.

The connections between William Crockett and the Elders go much further than the marriage license between Margaret Elder and David Crockett (b. 1779). On July 20, 1789, William Crockett [presumably Davy's uncle] issued a deed to Richard Featherston for land on the Catawba River in Lincoln County, North Carolina, which had been owned by a David Elder and witnessed by a John Patterson and a Robert Patterson.[213] In November 1792, William Crockett received a grant for land in Lincoln County, North Carolina, joining land of Robert Weir on headwaters of Kings Creek and adjoining Samuel Elder.[214]

---

210   Goodspeed, *History of East Tennessee*, 857.

211   Jones, *Crockett Cousins*, 10.

212   Dumplin Creek Baptist Church, Toomy.

213   Lincoln County, NC, Recorded Bk. 16, p. 359.

214   Lincoln County, NC, Recorded Bk. 2, p. 68.

A Samuel Elder received 150 acres from George Steel in Greene County in 1795.[215] There is a Samuel Elder in Greene County and later one in the Dumplin community where the Elder family's name is strongly associated.[216]

There are at least three contemporary David Crocketts in Davy's extended family. His uncle William Crockett had a son also named David Crockett. Born in 1779, it is almost certainly that this first cousin of Davy's was the person to whom the marriage license at the Jefferson County Courthouse was issued. It was this David Crockett who married a Margaret Elder, the daughter of David and Margaret Gordon Elder of the Dumplin community of Jefferson County, Tennessee, and it is this David and Margaret's marriage license that has been a part of Jefferson County history and misunderstanding for such a very long time. This David died September 28, 1851, in Gibson County, Tennessee.[217] This county was the last home of our subject Davy before he left for Texas. To add a further twist to an already confused issue, a daughter of David and Margaret Elder named Drucilla married another of David's first cousins, David B. Crockett (b. 1796, son of David's uncle Robert), in 1816.[218]

A clerk's copy of this marriage document hung in the courthouse in Dandridge for many years. A brouhaha began before 1950 when Harry Vance, the county clerk in whose office it hung, took it to his home. In a letter to Rick Farrar, County Court Clerk of Jefferson County, Margaret Vance Smith of Tampa, Florida, the daughter of the late Mr. Vance, stated that she was in possession of this document, given to her by her late father Harry Vance, who told her it was rescued and taken

---

215   Greene County Court Minutes April 21, 1795, Deed from Geo Steel for 150 acres. Attst John Jones [200 acres east side Lick Creek, Greene Co 1791] p. 409.

216   Samuel Elder in Greene County—Greene CCM 4/21/1795, p. 409, Deed from Geo Steel for 150 acres. Attst John Jones. Samuel Elder in Jefferson County—Listed as one of oldest members of Dumplin Baptist Church. Toomey

217   Jones, *Crockett Cousins*, 22.

218   Jones, *Crockett Cousins*, 52.

home by himself when Mr. Vance was throwing away obsolete documents that were taking up space in the clerk's office.[219] When Mrs. Smith decided to sell the document, Jefferson County was successful in getting a court ruling that the document was the lawful property of Jefferson County and the court ordered Mrs. Vance to surrender it to the county which she, after some legal battles, reluctantly did.

This controversy came to a head when Mrs. Smith decided to go on the PBS program *Antiques Roadshow* with the document to ascertain its value. Here is a transcription of the document's appearance on the show:

GUEST:

Because, you know, with things like this ... They become priceless when they're so unique and one of a kind.

PBS ANTIQUES ROADSHOW APPRAISER:

That's right. And to hang a price is very difficult.

GUEST:

I've never thought of a price.

ANTIQUES ROADSHOW APPRAISER:

It has, though, such historical significance to fill in these gaps in Crockett's life and to really be able to hold up a document that confirms all the speculations and wonderings about this activity in his life and when it took place. Because of that, we feel that it's worth $20,000 to $30,000.

---

219   Margaret Vance Smith of Tampa, FL. Letter to Rick Farrar, County Clerk, Jefferson County, TN, dated February 19, 2010.

November 07, 2011: After this segment aired in January 2006, a dispute about who legally owned this Crockett marriage license made news. As of July 2011, the Tennessee Court of Appeals upheld a trial court judgment that sided with Jefferson County in their case against *Antiques Roadshow* guest Margaret V. Smith. It was reported the license was returned to Jefferson County in 2010.[220]

In a letter from 1931, a member of the Elder family states, "Unfortunately 'the fair-haired Margaret' was not serious with her cousin. The tradition in our family is that they were cousins."[221] The confusion here is likely over the fact that the David Crockett who married Margaret was a first cousin of the more well-known David Crockett. This could account for the *tradition* that there were Elders and Crocketts who were cousins.

A story published in 1936: "The Elder Family. Elder, William— (1) William Elder, died May 13, 1817, probably near the town of Dandridge, Jefferson County, Tennessee, whither he had moved from western North Carolina, some time prior to 1800. It is believed that he is the William Elder who, in October 1805, was running a hotel at Dandridge, Tennessee." David Elder and Margaret Elder were children of William. "... copy of the field notes of Grant No. 24566 issued by the State of Tennessee November 15, 1841, calling for 5000 acres of land for the Epsom Salts Mfg Co..." in which David Elder was a 25 percent owner. "The land granted was situated on the South side of the French Broad River in Severe [*sic*] County, Tennessee not far from the town of Dandridge, where Davy Crockett was jilted by Margaret Elder." The marriage license for David and Margaret Elder is dated October 21, 1805, the same time that William Elder was supposed to be "running a hotel at Dandridge."[222]

---

220 Public Broadcasting Service, *Antiques Roadshow*, January 2006, David Crockett, Margaret Elder marriage license.

221 Miles M. Elder, Letter to the Tennessee State Library, May 14, 1931. In possession of the Tennessee State Library, Genealogy Dept.

222 *Southern Historical Research Magazine*. Vol. 1, no. 5, Nov 1936, p. 476–477.

In the same article stating that David's father lived about eight miles above Dandridge toward Morristown is the following, "Nearby was a tavern. ... A man named Elder managed the Tavern. He had two daughters ... Margaret ..."[223] The Elders are primarily associated with the Dumplin community that is sixteen miles southwest of Panther Springs and twenty-eight miles from John Crockett's home in Morristown. Dumplin is in the southwest corner of the county near where the War Trail entered Sevier County just west of Flat Gap. William Elder, Jefferson County records as a juror on July 30, 1797,[224] and again in September of 1815,[225] but no records could be found showing him as a property owner.

The Elder family has been associated with the Dumplin Creek Baptist Church since 1809 when Jacob Elder joined *by experience*. The will of one William Elder, dated June 10, 1823, mentions children James Elder and Samuel Elder "and the rest of my children Charles Elder, Martin Elder, Elijah Elder, Rebecca Elder and Rebecca Lawrence."[226]

David says that it was ten miles from the home of John Canaday at Panther Springs on the headwaters of Panther Creek [*N*, 51] to the home of his second love interest. The actual distance from Panther Springs to the little community of Dumplin is sixteen miles. David's ability to measure and recall distances, as previously cited, was almost always extremely accurate. It is highly unlikely that he would have missed the distance by six miles.

There is evidence of an early tavern in the Dumplin community not far from the Sevier County line. From the will of George Willcockson, dated April 16, 1799: "George Willcockson of the State of Tennessee and the county of Sevier ... to my son David Willcockson I give my

---

223 "Robert Henry Hynds." *The American Historical Magazine*, 298.

224 William Elder, Jefferson County records as a juror on July 30, 1797.

225 William Elder, Jefferson County records as a juror on Sept. of 1815.

226 Jefferson County Will Book 2, p. 413.

mill and Stills and the land and possessions to the fence above mill-dam and with the fence till it strikes the road that leads to William Goforth [the man from whom a William Crockett bought land in 1794] ... to my son George Willcockson I give my old plantation with the tavern and all my lands adjoining it."[227]

In a Knoxville newspaper article from the early 1900s, is the following account: "Comes a letter from one of the vice-presidents of the American Copper company, Goldfield, Nevada, ... The writer gives his name but prefers to be known only as M. B. A. ... It appears the redoubtable Davy swung the axe and cleared off a considerable acreage of native timber near Dandridge and for the lofty purpose of paying for his marriage license ... It further appears that after obtaining the coveted license he failed to negotiate the marriage through strenuous objection on the part of the lady's Pa. In the 90s of the last century [1890s] the unused license could be seen in the clerk's office at Dandridge."[228]

On David's way to see his second love interest, only days before their intended wedding, David decided to stop at a shooting match. He and a partner won, leaving him in such good humor that he was persuaded to participate in a full-fledged country frolic, delaying him substantially. It has been speculated that this episode of showing up hung over and days late for a visit with his intended and her family may have marked him as unreliable, and therefore not ideal as husband material.

> Just now I heard of a shooting-match in the neighbour-hood, right between where I lived and my girls house; and I determined to kill two birds with one stone, and to go to the shooting match first, and then to see her. I therefore made the Quaker believe I was going to hunt for deer, as they

---

227   Jefferson County Will Book 1, p. 82–84.

228   J. A. Dunn, *The Knoxville Journal*, c. 1898, Crockett Biography File, McClung Collection, Knoxville.

were pretty plenty about in those parts; but, instead of hunting them, I went straight on to the shooting-match, where I joined in with a partner, and we put in several shots for the beef. I was mighty lucky, and when the match was over I had won the whole beef. This was on a Saturday, and my success had put me in the finest humour in the world. So I sold my part of the beef for five dollars in the real grit. [*N*, 52]

David's second girlfriend had apparently indicated to David that she was interested in his offer of marriage, but her sister told him, soon before they were to be married, that "she was to be married to another man the next day" [N, 53]. There has been some speculation that his tardiness in getting to her home, because of his attendance at a shooting match, resulted in the bad news he received from her sister.[229] It seems highly unlikely that she could have come up with a new fiancée so quickly and decided to use this news as a way to rid herself of an undesirable suitor.

A ten-mile radius from John Canaday's home covers most of the primary communities within old Jeffereson County. Heading southeast it gets past Mossy Creek (Jefferson City today) almost to New Market, almost to Dandridge, past the headwaters of Long Creek neighborhood, past his father's tavern, and almost to Cheek's Crossroads.

---

229 Hauck, *Davy Crockett: A Handbook*, 14.

APPENDIX F:

The John L. Jacobs Account

Dated Nov 22, 1884:
Some weeks ago I saw in the Knoxville Chronicle an inquiry for the purpose of gaining knowledge of the history of the celebrated David Crockett. I first knew him when I was a child, then when a boy, then when a youth, perhaps 15 years old, then saw him when a man of 20 years.

Crockett was a poor man when first I saw him. He was then a married man, lived three-forths of a mile from my father in Findley's Gap, in Bays Mountain, Tenn.

This gap is on the road leading from Mossy Creek to Chucky, and is in the line of ridges that span the Honeycutt Valley that runs near to Morristown. My first recollection of Crockett was when a small boy of some 6 or 8 years [about 1810–1811]. He was then making rails for my father. I went to him where he had cut a very large yellow pine tree. He frequently called on me to hand him the wedge or glut, whichever he wanted. This ends my boyhood recollection of Crockett.

This period was near the time of the War of 1812. ... His wife's name was Mary Findley. When he left the country [1812], he was poor and left a debt of one dollar with my father.

He was absent several years before I saw him again. One morning I was standing in the door next to the main road. I looked down the road toward Mossy Creek and saw a fine looking man riding in front of a large drove of horses. He rode opposite me and stopped and asked if my mother was in the house. I answered she was.

'Tell her to come to the door.' I did so, and when she appeared he said, 'How do you do, Mrs. Jacobs?' My mother said, 'Sir, you have the advantage of me.' 'I am Davy Crockett,' he responded. 'Is that you, Davy?' said my mother. 'Yes,' said he, 'this is Davy Crockett.' Then a general shaking of hands took place and inquiry of the health of the families, etc.

Just at this moment his horses came rushing up and nearly got ahead of him. He thrust his hand into his pocket and pulled his pocket book out, took out a silver dollar and said, 'Here, Madam, is a dollar I owed to your husband, John Jacobs when I left the country.' My father had died in the meantime. My mother said, 'Davy I don't want it.' 'I owed it,' he said, 'and you have got to take it.' My mother then took the dollar and Davy Crockett rode on to South Carolina to sell his horses. This ends my second short acquaintance with this noted man. [Mr. Jacobs says he was "about 15" which would make the year about 1819–1820. His father had died about 1818.]

Some several years elapsed and Crockett made his way to the Congress of the United States [1827–1835]. James Blackburn had a cornshucking in my neighborhood. There were many hands around the heap. We saw a fine gentleman riding toward the house. He alighted and went into the house, made himself known, passed the usual compliments, then came down to the men around the heap of corn, gave a general shaking of hands with all the citizens, then turned up the cuffs of his fine broadcloth and went to shucking corn with the other hands.

He worked on until dinner was announced, then ate his dinner and left for his home. This was the last sight I ever had of this wonderful man. I shall here give you a description of Davy Crockett:

He was about six feet high, weighed about two hundred pounds, had no surplus flesh, broad shouldered, stood erect, was a man of great physical strength, of fine appearance, his cheeks mantled with a rosy hue, eyes vivacious, and in form, had no superior.

N.B. The writer studied whether to write or not. After serious and close thinking, I could find no-one in all that part of your country that had any recollection of Davy Crockett but myself. This prompted me to write. I am now entering into my 80th year [born circa 1804]. I never knew where Crockett was born.

APPENDIX G:

A Finley Compendium

Scottish Heritage of the Finleys

The Finleys, like the Crocketts, were Ulster-Scots who scraped out a living with only the most basic of life's necessities. According to some undocumented accounts, William (also known as *Billy*) Finley, the father of Polly, was born April 11, 1765, and married Jean Kennedy.

Making a solid link for individual Ulster-Scots families back to Scotland is not usually easily accomplished, if possible at all. Clan Fionnladh, to which the Finley family is associated, is generally located in Perthshire, Scotland.

1. Alexander Finley; b. 1667, Inshervie, Fife; m. Margaret Jennings; d. 1742; their son:

2. James Finley; b. 1687, in Scotland, taken to Ireland; m. Elizabeth Patterson, 1706; landed at New Castle, Delaware, 1720; d. 1753, in Cumberland County, Pennsylvania; their son:

3. John Finley; m. Thankful Doak; their son:

4. John Finley, Jr.; b. 1724, in Pennsylvania; m. Mary Caldwell, 1741; their son:

5. John Caldwell Finley; b. 1742; m. Ann Miller; their son:

6. William Finley, b. 1765; m. Jean Kennedy, 1786; their daughter:

7. Mary [Polly] Finley, 1788–1815, first wife of David Crockett.

Identifying the family of William Finley and his wife Jean/Jane Kennedy Finley has not been an easy task although many people over many years have spent time trying to connect them. In the last will and testament of William Finley, his wife is referred to as "Jean." On a State of Tennessee Grant #220 in June of 1824, she is called "Jean." On an indenture document for Jenny Bell in September of 1816, she is listed as "Jane," and in a document relating to the estate of John Sterling, a neighbor, in April of 1819, a Jane Finley was a buyer of estate items. On the land grant and the will of her deceased husband, her name is listed as Jean, and these documents should carry more weight because they are attested by witnesses who were neighbors known to her and the Finley family.

John Caldwell Finley appears to be the likely father of William Finley, Polly Finley Crockett's father. The problem has been that there were a number of Finleys in East Tennessee during this early settlement period. There were men by the name of *William Finley* living at the same time in counties of Blount, Greene, Hawkins, and Jefferson in East Tennessee.

Contentious Finley Court Case

A court case involving John Finley offers a glimpse of the neighborhood of the Finleys and seems to have drawn sides between friends of the Finleys and others who lived in the neighborhood. John Finley filed a case of slander against David Givens, Richard Grace, and William Bradshaw by his attorney Adam Peck in 1811. The case was heard by Judge James Trimble. Grace, Bradshaw, and Givens were accused of spreading the word that John Finley had committed the crime of buggery on a mare belonging to Bradshaw in October of 1810. Two hundred bushels of corn were paid to William and James Finley, heirs of John Finley, in 1815 after his death. Jefferson County Court Minutes for August 1799, Book 1, page 146, records "David Givens was bound by indenture to William Bradshaw until he arrive at the age of twenty one." In one of the affidavits for the case it was said that John Finley had considered moving to the Duck and Elk River area in order to avoid prosecution on the buggery charge. [Jeff Circuit Court Loose Documents]

The following looks to be the best available data on this William Finley and his family:

John Caldwell Finley

b. 11 JAN 1741/42 in Augusta County, VA
d. 1818 in Homestead, Gaston County, NC
Christening: 24 JAN 1741/42 Tinkling Springs, Augusta County, VA
Father: John Finley, Jr., b. 28 DEC 1724 in East Nottingham, Chester, PA
Mother: Mary Thankful Caldwell, b. 1728 in Charlottesville, VA
Marriage 1 Ann Miller, b. 1742
Married: 10 APR 1762, Lincoln Co., NC
Children
1. Mary Finley, b. 25 JAN 1763 in Lincoln Co., NC
2. William Finley, b. 11 APR 1765 in Lincoln Co., NC
3. John Finley, b. 17 FEB 1767 in Lincoln Co., NC
4. Agnes Finley, b. 20 OCT 1769 in Lincoln Co., NC
5. David Finley, b. 22 MAY 1770 in Lincoln Co., NC
6. Alexander Finley, b. 10 AUG 1772 in Lincoln Co., NC
7. James Finley, b. 10 MAR 1774 in Lincoln Co., NC
8. Osborne Finley, b. 1776
9. Daughter Finley, b. 1778
10. Robert Miller Finley, b. 18 SEP 1782 in Gaston Co., NC

In naming their children, William and Jean Finley used the same names above for their children: Mary, William, John, David, and James.

Married Women Named Kennedy

According to family records, John Finley, born 1767, lived near enough to the Battle of Kings Mountain to have heard the battle and, at age twelve, went to participate in it. The fact that both John Finley, born 1767 and William, born 1765, above, married women named Kennedy perhaps indicates that the illusive Kennedy/Canady family might be located somewhere near their home in Lincoln County, North Carolina. It also strengthens the case that William of Jefferson County and John who married Margaret Elizabeth Kennedy are brothers; in that time, brothers often married sisters from their home neighborhoods.[230]

Robert Sevier

Robert Sevier, brother of John Sevier, was wounded at the Battle of Kings Mountain. "With his nephew and other men of his company, he spent the night in the home of John Finley, a Patriot who lived nearby. Joseph Sevier oldest son of John Sevier, later married Mary Finley of this family."[231] Here again is information that helps to locate the home of John Finley as being very near the battlefield at Kings Mountain.

History of Finleys on Bays Mountain and Finley Gap

The Finley family must have moved into their home in the gap of Bays Mountain at a fairly early date. The name of the gap, Finley Gap, is still in use today though the association with Crockett seems to have been lost in recent years. The naming of a topographic landmark for

---

230   Jefferson County Deeds, Volume B, page 46.

231   Goodspeed, *History of East Tennessee*, 857.a

a family who lived in close proximity was common. The early use of the Finley name in association with the gap would indicate an early habitation there.

The earliest entry for William Finley in the records of the Jefferson County Court is in May 1796, when he was exempted from payment of a poll tax.[232] These exemptions were usually made for those over age fifty (William was likely not that old), those who were disabled in some way, or those who were too poor to pay it. It is most likely the latter category was the reason for William's exemption. Again in November 1797, the County Court "Ordered that a Jury view and lay off a road from Finley's in the gap to the iron workd at Mossy Creek. Vz James Reece, William Finley, Isaac Newman, Christopher Haynes, John Bradshaw, William Line."[233] This 1797 reference establishes that the Finleys had located at Finley Gap by 1797. The Finley one-hundred-acre tract began in the gap with a narrow neck that reached out to the old road and then extended on into the flat bottom land of the Dumplin Creek valley.

Settlers often would live on a piece of land for a considerable time prior to the actual completion of the purchase and registration. These transactions were known as *occupant claims*. There is no registration for land in Jefferson County for William Finley until 1814 when he recorded one hundred acres in the "gap of the knobs." The entry was a part of a transfer from Archibald Roane to John Hays in a five-hundred-acre tract which had taken place in 1808 and not surveyed until March of 1813.[234] This certainly is the Finley homestead land.

David says in the *Narrative* that he and Polly, after their marriage, lived on a rented farm near the Finleys. When the sites are viewed, it is possible to see one house site from the other. It was difficult to

---

232   Jones, *Crockett Cousins*, 10.

233   Dumplin Creek Baptist Church, Toomy.

234   Lincoln County, NC Recorded Bk 16, p. 359.
      Lincoln County, NC Recorded Bk. 2, p. 68.
      Greene County Court Minutes April 21, 1795, Deed from Geo Steel for 150 acres.
      Attst John Jones [200 acres east side Lick Creek, Greene Co 1791] p. 409.

imagine how they could be on two different parcels being in such close proximity on the same road. The locations and the account gave the impression that perhaps David did not want to admit that he had lived on the same property as his in-laws, but once again his account is cleared by the documented facts.

The place and time of the wedding of Polly Finley's parents is obscure as is their home prior to moving to Jefferson County, Tennessee. Even the first and last name of Polly's mother is confused.

William and Jean Finley had eight known children. They were sons John, James, William, Samuel, and David and daughters Mary (Polly), Jean, and Susannah. To date no information has been obtained on the family of Jean Kennedy Finley. In his will of April 3, 1818, William Finley leaves his one-hundred-acre farm and homestead to his son "Kannedy" and to his wife in a life estate. This son is mentioned three more times; in these three instances, the spelling is "Kaneday." Records indicate that John Finley had died by June 13, 1814, with administrators named as James Findley and William Findley and security provided by James Findley, William Findley, Reuben Churchman, and Thomas McCuistion.

Jean Finley seemed to imply that Polly was the oldest of the children when she explained to David the reason for her hostility toward the marriage (after she had resigned herself to the fact): "she came to me and looked at me mighty good, and asked my pardon for what she had said, and invited me to stay. She said it was the first child she had ever had to marry" [N, 66]. Some evidence points toward two of her brothers being older than she. A person very likely to be her brother James witnessed a deed in 1805. If he were required to be *of age* to do so, he would likely have had to have been born sometime before 1786. William Finley, Sr., and William Finley, Jr., witnessed a deed in 1806 and by the same reasoning William, Jr. would have been born around the same time.

Mary (Polly), according to an account within the Flowers family, was born January 4, 1787, and the same account says that she died "June 11, 1815." William probably married Jean sometime prior to

1784. The inscription on William's grave marker, put there in 1964, gives a birth date of "Circa 1750." The original hand-wrought field-stone says "W. Finley d. 1819." It is likely that the date of birth of April 11, 1765, is very close to a date that makes sense. Of the Finley daughters, Jean married a John Barnes in 1815 and Susannah married a Parks in 1818.

A list of the estate of David's father-in-law, William Finley, gives some insight into the extent of this Ulster-Scots's accumulation of possessions in a lifetime of farming on the early western frontier:

> Four head of horses seven head of cattle twenty head of hogs seven head of ducks one syth and cradle seven head of gees one funnel two little wheels one washing tub one big wheel one cart one smoothing Iron three bed steads and beds and beding some shoe maker tools one table four crocks one fir-kin one razor and shaving box four chairs and one fraim two fat geards two reels one hogshead one meat tub one cutting knife and box two churns three barrels two bee stands two pair drawing gears three pails one Iron wedge nine pew-ter plates and one dish two empty bee stands ten spoons one loom two pair of temples six reeds six knives and forks three pair of geers one quill wheel one looking glass four pair of chards ploough clevises five tin cups and one quart and one pitcher one coffy pot one tin pan two candle sticks two baskets one sifter one half bushel one tarr bucket one tray fifteen worping spools two bells three augers and one gouge one draw knife one howel one inshave one crow two plain locks one matic two broad hoes three ploughs two axs one oven one iron pot and two pair of pot hooks one chest and dresser one pair of warping bars and spool fraim nine sheep two bags.

William Finley's Last Will and Testament

A glimpse into the lives of the earliest settlers can be seen in the records of their passing, their last wills and testaments. What follows is the recorded Last Will and Testament of David Crockett's father-in-law, William Finley, father to Mary (Polly) Finley Crockett. At the time the will was made, Finley's daughter, David Crockett's wife, had died leaving three grandchildren of William Finley referenced in the will below.

William Finley's Will, April 3rd, 1818

In the name of God amen.

I Wiliam Finley of the County of Jefferson state of Tenessee Weak in body but sound and perfect of mind and memory blessed be almity God for the same do make and publish this my last Wil and Testament in maner and form folowing. First I give and bequeath to my son James my large pot rack I also give and bequeath to my sons Wiliam and Samuel the sum of two dol-lars each and I do give to my two daughters Jean Barnes and Susana Parks the sum of two dolars each. I do also give to my daughter Mary [Polly] Crockets three children John, Wiliam, and Poly two dolars each which said several Legacies or sums of money I wil and order shal be paid to the said Respective Legacies with in twelve months after my decease. I further give and devise to my son Kanedy his heirs and assigns the land and plantation whereon I now live Containing one hundred acres to hold to him the said Kaneday his heirs and assigns forever with this reserve that my wife Jean shall live In the house whare I now live during her life. I give and bequeath to my wife Jean and my son Kaneday all my beds and house furniture. My horses cattle hogs and lastly as to all the real and remainder of my personal estate goods and chatels of what kind and native dowry I give and bequeath the same to my beloved wife and son Kaneday and I appoint my wife Jean Executrix and my son Kaneday Executor, of this my last will and testament. I hereby revoke in all former wills by me made. In witness whereof I have here unto set my hand and seal the third day of April in the year of our Lord one thousand eight hundred and eighteen. Signed sealed published and declared by the above named Wiliam Finley to be the last Will and Testament in the presence of us here- unto subscribe do ournames as witness the presence of the Testation

Andrew McCuistion, James McCuistion, Richard X Grisham, his mark

Signed: William Finley seal

In the will Andrew McCuistion, James McCuistion, and Richard Grisham were all neighbors of the Finleys who lived over the ridge in Finley Gap less than two miles southeast of William Finley's house. They were located on the headwaters of the Long Creek neighborhood near the top of Bays Mountain. James McCuistion acquired David Crockett's rifle when David left Jefferson County for middle Tennessee around 1812. According to McCuistion family tradition, James McCuistion operated a kind of neighborhood store out of his home and Crockett owed him for items bought at the store on credit. About this time there began a migration to the fertile and game-rich Duck and Elk River country around Winchester, Tennessee. When David decided to move to that area near the end of 1811, he gave James McCuistion his rifle in payment or partial payment of the bill he owed at the store.

William Finley Married Jean Kennedy

According to the Torrence and Whittenburg's genealogical work, William Finley married Jean Kennedy in 1786 in Lincoln County, North Carolina. The bulk of the evidence for Jean's lineage seems to rest upon the name of the youngest son, spelled three times in the William Finley will, *Kaneday*. When looking for sons who remained in Jefferson County after the death of William, none are found with the names of James, William, or Samuel. Also not found are any Finleys by the name of *Kaneday, Kennedy,* or similar spellings.

What is found is a David *C.* Finley who obtained land grants adjacent to the William Finley property in Finley Gap. The marriage records of Jefferson County show that a "David *Canady* Finley" married Sally Lankford on September 25, 1819. The marriage was performed by Rueben Churchman, a Justice of the Peace and Finley neighbor, and the bond was given by Samuel Finley, presumably David Finley's brother.

This leads us to a rather curious possibility. David C. Finley must be the youngest son of William and Jean by virtue of his land grants adjacent to the original Finley property that he now owned. If this David C. Finley is indeed *Kaneday* Finley, then the spelling of his middle name may not begin with a *K* but with a *C*, and the name could be *Canaday*. This would certainly be consistent with the phonetic spellings in the William Finley will.

Once again the world of the early nineteenth century seems to become awfully small. Could Jean Finley be related to the family of Quaker John Canaday? It is a long way from a certainty, but it is a tantalizing coincidence if not.

John Canaday

Apparently John Canaday and his son Charles owned land quite close to the Finley farm. One of John's deeds calls for 230 acres, part of which lay "on the waters of cedar pond" and bordered Charles Canaday, Samuel Jackson, and Solomon Cox. The cedar pond and the poplar pond are mentioned in the 1836 Civil District Survey of Jefferson County in Finley Gap. They are two natural ponds that lie half a mile apart. The poplar pond was just across the Chucky Pike road from the location of the Finley home at what is today known as Collier's Corner (the intersection of the Dumplin Valley Road and the Chucky Pike).

This property was some eight miles from John Canaday's home at Panther Springs. John Canaday's Long Hole Mill site, acquired later, was less than five miles as the crow flies from Finley Gap. Samuel Jackson was also located at Panther Springs and Solomon Cox was a fellow Quaker who had established himself, in 1798, "on the south side of the Holston River in the nobs joining the Barrens" (Bays Mountain) and in 1809 in the "Honey Cut Valley." The Hunnicutt Valley comes right up to the William Finley tract. All these references serve to establish a connection between Quaker John Canaday at Panther Springs and others with whom he was associated in the Finley Gap area. His knowledge of the area and its residents quite possibly prompted his admonition to David not to join in with the "great deal of bad company" there [N, 33].

Could his judgment concerning these people possibly be skewed by his knowledge of, and relationship with, Jean Finley? Could Jean be a former Quaker from the family who *married out* and had joined the heathen Scots-Irish, thus making David's association with them a cause for such an admonition from John Canaday to stay away from them?

Gravesite of William Finley

On the Quarles farm in the Dumplin Valley near the headwaters of Dumplin Creek, less than a mile from where David and the Finleys lived, is the gravesite of David's father-in-law, William Finley. The will of William Finley is dated April 3, 1818. The will was presented to the county court in the June session of 1819. The original fieldstone grave marker is inscribed "W. Finley, Died 1818."

A marker placed at the Finley gravesite by the Association for the Preservation of Tennessee Antiquities states, "William (Billy) Finley, [Born] About 1750 [probably more like 1760–63]—[Died] 1819. Father of Polly Finley, wife of David Crockett. Legendary descendant of Scottish King MacBeth. Erected jointly by Jefferson-Hamblen County Chapters ATPA — 1964." The cemetery is located on the Quarles farm just east of Finley Gap in the Dumplin Valley.

For some years before the Quarles family acquired the property where the cemetery is located, the land had been cultivated. Encroachment on the burying ground resulted in the remaining stones from the cemetery being all piled onto the grave of William Finley. Indications are that approximately twenty-five graves were located in the burying ground around William's grave. Mrs. Quarles searched through the pile of stones for other inscriptions, but found none. The Finley fieldstone was discovered by a descendent that came there from out of state to search for his ancestor's grave in the 1950s. William Finley's stone is broken in three places but has been repaired. The stone is unique among the other stones in the burying ground for its thickness and shape. It is made from gray limestone, is about 4" in thickness, about 14" wide, and 24" tall. It has a graceful rounded arch at the top that creates flat ledges where it meets its square sides. The inscription on the stone is fading rapidly and will be unreadable soon.

Other Early History ... War Path 1776

Indications are that a sizeable number of the earliest settlers first saw these lands while accompanying Col. William Christian in August 1776 on his expedition against the Cherokees. That campaign involved some eighteen hundred soldiers who followed the War Path to the Cherokee towns to punish the Cherokees for their efforts against the settlements in aid of the British. An Indian trader named Isaac Thomas was the guide and several of the men known to have been on this expedition returned to settle on lands they had traversed. It is quite possible that John Crockett was among the soldiers. The route took them right down Long Creek to its source on the south side of Bays Mountain and over the mountain near Finley Gap to the Dumplin Creek valley which followed on to the southwest. There is good evidence that Samuel Lyle was on that trek and the route traveled directly over lands he was to settle on the headwaters of Long Creek some eight years later. This is the neighborhood of the Finley family and where David and Polly lived for almost six years after their marriage.

This neighborhood encompassed both sides of Bays Mountain. Along the east side was the headwaters of Long Creek and across the mountain was the Finley Gap and Dumplin Valley neighborhood. David and Polly lived in this neighborhood for six or so years near the Finleys after their marriage. At the top of Bays Mountain at Finley Gap were John and Rebecca Jacobs and family. Around them were Jerimiah Nicholson; Patrick McGuire; James, Robert, Thomas, Andrew, and Joseph McCuistion; Andrew McAdow; Samuel Lyle; Daniel Lyle; and John Blackburn.

Finleys Not on the Tax List

It is interesting to note that in a list of Tennessee taxpayers for Jefferson County in the year 1800, the following persons are listed in Captain Harmon's Co. This list should have included the area where the Finleys lived, although they are not listed anywhere in the tax list: Samuel Bradshaw (630 acres), William Bradshaw (245 acres), James Bradshaw (800 acres), William Churchman, John Canaday Sr. and Jr., Charles Canaday, Porter Canaday, John Cluck, Peter Cluck, Richard Grace, Christopher Hanes (8000 acres), John Longacre (427 acres), Benjamin Longacre (397 acres), and Samuel Jackson (5000 acres).

Of these area residents we know that William Bradshaw, Benjamin Longacre, and Richard Grace were living along the same north side of Bays Mountain just west of the Finleys. The Clucks are believed to have owned property adjacent to the Finleys on the east side.

A list of Captain Carson's Company (that contains some residents from Finley Gap but appears to be folks mostly on the west side of

Bays Mountain) contains many familiar names from the area associated with the Finleys: Henry Bradford, John Blackburn, Elizabeth Corbet, Richard Grisham, Patrick Gibbons, Samuel and David Lyle, Hugh Martin, Benjamin McFarland, Patrick McGuire, Andrew McAdoo, Jeremiah Nicholson, Patrick McGuire, the McCuistions (Joseph, Robert, Thomas, David, Andrew, and James), Jeremiah Nicholson, Joseph Prigmore, the Rankins, and John Sterling.[235]

The two groups make up the neighborhood area all around the Finley property but without listing the Finleys.

---

235 *Southern Historical Research Magazine.* Vol. 1, No. 5, Nov 1936, p. 476-47

About the Author

Joe Swann has spent the greater part of his life researching and documenting the history of David Crockett's life in East Tennessee. The spark behind this book is the David Crockett Rifle that has been in the author's family since 1800.

Swann was born in East Tennessee and graduated from the University of Tennessee in 1972. He was appointed by the Governor to the Tennessee Historical Commission from 2010 to 2020 and served on the body's historical markers committee. Swann has been a member of the East Tennessee Historical Society for more than 20 years and served as its president from 1999–2002. Swann has done numerous presentations on David Crockett's life in East Tennessee.

Authors who have used research provided by Swann include:
- Michael Wallis author of *The Lion of the West*: "The voice and vision of Joe Swann echoes throughout much of this book."
- Cameron Judd, author of *Crockett of Tennessee*, who has published more than thirty historical and western novels and is an award-winning journalist.